高职高专"十二五"部委级规划教材

纺织专业英语

李建萍　主编

化学工业出版社

·北京·

本书是高职高专院校纺织类或纺织贸易类专业英语课程的项目化教材，包括纤维原料、纺纱、机织、针织、非织造、洗涤标签与纺织标准等11个项目；每个项目均设计了学习目标、文献阅读、专业词汇、思考题和实践作业，涵盖了纺织专业常用的基本词汇，实用性强。本书配备了不少插图，方便读者阅读理解。教材内容参考英美的原版教材，语言流畅。

本书既可作为高职高专院校现代纺织技术、纺织品检测与贸易及相关专业的专业英语教材，又可作为纺织贸易从业人员的自学参考书。

图书在版编目（CIP）数据

纺织专业英语/李建萍主编．—北京：化学工业出版社，2014.1（2024.8重印）
高职高专"十二五"部委级规划教材
ISBN 978-7-122-19104-5

Ⅰ.①纺⋯ Ⅱ.①李⋯ Ⅲ.①纺织-英语-高等职业教育-教材 Ⅳ.①H31

中国版本图书馆CIP数据核字（2013）第279612号

责任编辑：崔俊芳　　　　　　　　　　文字编辑：林　媛
责任校对：徐贞珍　　　　　　　　　　装帧设计：关　飞

出版发行：化学工业出版社（北京市东城区青年湖南街13号　邮政编码100011）
印　　装：北京盛通数码印刷有限公司
787mm×1092mm　1/16　印张8　字数175千字　2024年8月北京第1版第7次印刷

购书咨询：010-64518888　　　　　　　售后服务：010-64518899
网　　址：http://www.cip.com.cn
凡购买本书，如有缺损质量问题，本社销售中心负责调换。

定　　价：26.00元　　　　　　　　　　　　　　　　　　版权所有　违者必究

前　言

本教材是在 2005 年版的《纺织专业英语》教材基础上进行修订编写。此教材一直在多所院校现代纺织技术、纺织品检验与贸易、服用材料设计与应用、针织与针织服装等专业使用。为了配合国家骨干院校建设重点项目"现代纺织技术专业"教学改革以及教育部扶持项目"纺织品检验与贸易专业"的课程改革，对原书进行了修订，以便于项目化教学的实施。

此次修订打破了原书的课文形式，结构上以项目化为导向，把教学内容划分成若干项目，每个项目的内容编写按照四个方面进行：学习目标、文献阅读、专业词汇、思考题和实践作业。

学习目标：为本项目要掌握的知识点和要达到的技能，在这一目标驱动下，激发学生读懂英文资料、学习知识的兴趣。

文献阅读：为精选的纺织英文文章，着重于生产和贸易中常遇到的知识，提高学生阅读英文资料的能力。

专业词汇：对本项目中应该掌握的专业词汇归纳总结，便于学生学习。

思考题和实践作业：对作业形式进行改革，把原来的单纯书面作业改革成书面作业和实际调研考察相结合，并以团队为单位完成英文报告。这样更有助于提高学生的实践能力、分析问题能力、英文应用能力和团队合作精神。

全书由 11 个部分组成，分别为绪论、天然纤维素纤维、天然蛋白质纤维、再生纤维素纤维、合成纤维、纱线、纺纱加工、机织与机织物、针织与针织物、非织造布、洗涤标签与纺织标准。通过深入企业调研，了解到企业以及商检部门必须具备的知识，对原书的内容做了调整，增加新型纺织材料、纺织标准等内容，使教材内容更全面、更新颖、更实用。

本教材编写团队由长期从事纺织专业英语教学的教师和资深行业工作人员组成，教师都具有丰富的教学经验，并具备双师素质及职业技能考评员资格，熟悉行业职业标准及岗位要求。

本教材由成都纺织高等专科学校李建萍主编。第 1 章～第 5 章、第 9 章、第 10 章由李建萍编写，第 6 章、第 7 章由成都纺织高等专科学校耿亮编写，第 8 章由李建萍和沙洲职业工学院于勤编写，第 11 章由汉中出入境检验检疫局蓝海啸编写。全书由李建萍统稿。

欢迎广大读者对本书提出宝贵意见和建议。

编　者

2013 年 10 月

Contents / 目录

- **Chapter One General Introduction / 绪论** ——————— 1
    - 1.1 Introduction to Textile / 纺织概论 ……………… 2
    - 1.2 Textile Fibers and Their Properties / 纺织纤维及性能 ……… 4
- **Chapter Two Natural Cellulosic Fiber / 天然纤维素纤维** ——— 11
    - 2.1 Cotton / 棉 ……………………………… 12
    - 2.2 Bast Fiber / 韧皮纤维 ……………………… 15
- **Chapter Three Natural Protein Fibers / 天然蛋白质纤维** ——— 21
    - 3.1 Wool / 羊毛 ……………………………… 22
    - 3.2 Specialty Animal Fibers / 特种动物毛 ……………… 24
    - 3.3 Silk / 蚕丝 ……………………………… 26
- **Chapter Four Manufactured Cellulosic Fibers / 再生纤维素纤维** ——— 31
    - 4.1 Rayon / 黏胶纤维 ………………………… 32
    - 4.2 Acetate / 醋酯纤维 ………………………… 33
    - 4.3 A New Type of Manufactured Cellulosic Fiber-Lyocell / 新型再生纤维素纤维——莱赛尔纤维 ……………… 34
- **Chapter Five Synthetic Fibers / 合成纤维** ——————— 37
    - 5.1 Polyamide Fibers / 聚酰胺纤维 ……………… 38
    - 5.2 Polyester Fibers / 聚酯纤维 ………………… 39
    - 5.3 Polyacrylic Fibers / 聚丙烯腈纤维 …………… 40
    - 5.4 Polyvinyl Chloride Fibers / 聚氯乙烯纤维 ……… 41
    - 5.5 Polyvinyl Alcohol Fibers / 聚乙烯醇纤维 ……… 41
    - 5.6 Polyolefin Fibers / 聚烯烃纤维 ……………… 41
    - 5.7 Spandex Fiber / 氨纶 ……………………… 42
    - 5.8 Aramid / 芳纶 ……………………………… 43
- **Chapter Six Yarn / 纱线** ——————————— 45
    - 6.1 Classification of Yarns / 纱线分类 …………… 46

6.2　Structure and Characteristics / 纱线结构与性能 ……………………… 54

Chapter Seven　Yarn Manufacturing / 纺纱加工 ——— 61
　　7.1　History of Yarn / 纱线的发展史 ……………………………………… 62
　　7.2　Traditional Spinning / 传统纺纱 ……………………………………… 62
　　7.3　Modification of Ring Spinning / 环锭纺纱改造 ……………………… 66
　　7.4　New Methods of Spinning System / 新型纺纱 ……………………… 69

Chapter Eight　Weaving and Woven Fabrics / 机织与机织物 ——— 77
　　8.1　Introduction to Fabrics / 织物概述 …………………………………… 78
　　8.2　Construction of Woven Fabrics / 机织物结构 ………………………… 78
　　8.3　The Three Basic Weaves / 三原组织 ………………………………… 79
　　8.4　Weaving Process / 机织过程 ………………………………………… 81
　　8.5　Technical Parameters of Woven fabrics / 机织物结构参数 ………… 88

Chapter Nine　Knitting and Knit Fabrics / 针织与针织物 ——— 93
　　9.1　Terms of Knitting and Knit Fabric / 针织和针织物的基本术语 …… 94
　　9.2　Weft Knitting / 纬编 …………………………………………………… 94
　　9.3　Warp Knitting / 经编 …………………………………………………… 96

Chapter Ten　Nonwoven Fabric / 非织造布 ——— 99
　　10.1　Dry-lay Webs / 干法成网 …………………………………………… 100
　　10.2　Wet-lay Webs / 湿法成网 …………………………………………… 101

Chapter Eleven　Care Labels and Textile Standards / 洗涤标签与纺织标准 ——— 105
　　11.1　Care Labels / 洗涤标签 ……………………………………………… 106
　　11.2　Textile Standards / 纺织标准 ………………………………………… 111

Reading Material 1　Textured Yarns / 变形纱 ——— 115

Reading Material 2　New Types of Loom / 新型织机 ——— 117

Reading Material 3　Mechanical Bonding / 机械固结 ——— 119

Reference / 参考文献 ——— 121

Chapter One
General Introduction / 绪论

Objectives / 学习目标：

1. Introduce the development of textile industry.

2. State the definition of textile fiber, and describe the classification of textile fibers.

3. To describe primary and secondary properties of fibers and their relationships to end-use performance.

1.1 Introduction to Textile / 纺织概论

The word textile comes from the Latin term textilis ("woven", and the verb textere, "to weave"). Today the word textile is more generalized to refer to products made from fibers. A fiber is defined, in a very general way, as any product (capable of being woven or otherwise made into a fabric). It may be thought of as the smallest visible unit of textile production. These definitions are quite broad, and it is often difficult for a textile technologist to delineate what is and is not a fiber or a textile.

Fibers (the usual starting place for a study of textiles) may be agricultural products (such as cotton or wool) or units (such as nylon or polyester) manufactured in a chemical plant. Fibers then serve as the raw material in the next stage of textile manufacturing. They may be spun into a strand, called a yarn, that can be used to knit a sweater, to sew two pieces of fabric together, or to weave a fabric. Fibers also may be made directly into a broad range of nonwoven fabrics such as felt for a hat or the underlayment for a modern highway.

Fabric is a planar structure produced by interlacing yarns in processes such as weaving, knitting, knotting, and braiding, or by binding fibers together to form a structure. Fabrics are produced in such forms as the flat sheets for a bed, the tubular body of a T-shirt, or the shaped nose cone of a rocket. Many of these fabrics are not aesthetically pleasing during the early stages of their manufacture. To enhance their appearance and improve their functional performance, fabrics can be dyed or printed, then treated with special finishes. The result is called dyed and finished fabric.

Understanding the broad variety of textile products available requires systematic study. This textbook introduces such a study by first categorizing products as fibers, yarns, fabrics, and dyed and finished textiles. Within these product classes, textiles are described by their primary end uses, most frequently by the primary textile markets: apparel, domestic, and industrial. The delineation of the products within these market categories is not precise. Some statistics include all clothing products in the apparel classification; others place protective clothing and military uniforms in the industrial textile category. Domestic, or household, textiles include such products as towels, sheets, draperies, upholstery, and some carpets and rugs. The industrial textile market encompasses products as diverse as tire cord, filters, automotive upholstery, hot air balloons, and parachutes. Carpets and floor coverings are such a large market in both the industrial and household sectors that the figures for floor coverings frequently are segregated as a fourth primary textile market.

The textile properties of concern to the consumer in each of these markets are likely to be quite different. For some apparel textiles, color and style may be more important than durability and requirements for care. Color and moisture absorbency may be important criteria to a consumer selecting a bath towel. Durability, mechanical properties, and price may be the important criteria to the purchasing officer responsible for selecting the cord to be used in manufacturing tires.

Traditionally, the textile and apparel industries had consisted of small firms competing vigorously. Economics textbooks often used them as examples of perfect competition. By the 1940s some firms had been consolidated in an effort to increase profits through economies of scale. In the 1950s, J. Sencer Love began to acquire the firms that would become Burlington Industries. Thirty years later, in the 1980s, Burlington Industries and its competitors were restructured through mergers, acquisitions, and leveraged buyouts. Changes in ownership and in the corporate structure of the major textile firms are expected to continue into the 1990s.

After the consolidation of the industry in the 1940s and 1950s, manufacturing productivity increased. Individual firms gained control of a larger share of the market and concentrated their production efforts in specific areas. Larger firms could afford to modernize production facilities and to fund new product development. Recent modernizations have focused on the installation of highly automated equipment that reduces the number of employees in production areas.

Traditionally, the textile and apparel industries were referred to as labor-intensive rather than capital-intensive. The basic machines used for textile and apparel production were relatively inexpensive, but they required large numbers of skilled and semiskilled workers to keep them operating. Labor was cheap and plentiful in the textile-producing states. The number of people employed by the textile industry in the United States has decreased in recent years. Employment dropped from 709,000 in July 1990 to 667,000 in July 1991. The automation of the industry and increased importing of textiles from overseas are responsible for many of the changes in employment figures. The skill level of employees is changing as well, because workers responsible for highly automated equipment must receive special training.

Just as changes in textile manufacturing have occurred over the years, so has textile consumption changed. Between 1950 and 1955, the average worldwide cotton fiber consumption was 17,839,680 pounds. The United States was the major consumer, followed by western Europe, eastern Europe, China, India, and Japan. Between 1985 and 1989, average cotton consumption was 39,760,320 pounds per year. China was the major consumer, followed by eastern Europe, India, United States, Western Europe, Pakistan, and Brazil. The world economy is changing and the textile industry is at the forefront of that change.

In 1980s, fiber consumption in the United States increased 9 percent. Wool consumption increased 50 percent; cotton, almost 33 percent; manufactured fibers, 6.5 percent; and other fibers decreased 57 percent.

1.2　Textile Fibers and Their Properties / 纺织纤维及性能

1.2.1　The Classification of Textile Fibers / 纤维分类

Fibers, the primary materials from which most textile products are made, can be defined as units of hairlike dimensions, with a length at least one hundred times greater than the width. Many substances found in nature can be classified as fibers according to this definition. However, only a limited number of these materials are useful in the production of yarns and fabrics.

As is known to all of us, textile fibers may be found in nature or created by man. Those that are found in nature are known as natural fibers, which are taken from either animal, vegetable, or mineral sources. Animal fibers could be further subdivided into those fibers from the hair of an animal such as wool and those from an extruded web such as silk. Plant fibers could be further subdivided according to the part of the plant that produces the fiber: the leaf, a hair produced from a seedpod, or the stem. The latter are called bast fibers. Chemically, the classification might be protein for animal fibers, cellulosic for plant fibers, and names of the specific minerals (such as asbestos) for mineral fibers. Using this scheme, wool is an animal, hair, or protein fiber and cotton is a plant, seedpod, or cellulosic fiber.

Those that are created by man through technology are known as man-made fibers, which are subdivided into two basic classifications. Regenerated man-made fibers are made from natural materials that cannot be used for textiles in their original form, but that can be regenerated into usable fibers by chemical treatment and processing. These regenerated fibers are made from such divers substances as wood, corn, protein, small cotton bits called linters, and seaweed. True synthetic man-made fibers are made or "synthesized" completely from chemical substances such as petroleum derivatives. And it was not until 1885, when the first man-made fiber Rayon was produced commercially that man began to make use of both the natural fiber and the man-made fiber to produce textile products.

1.2.2　The Main Properties of Textile Fibers / 纺织纤维的主要性能

1.2.2.1　The Primary Properties of Textile Fibers / 纺织纤维的基本性能

Whether a fiber can be utilized in the creation of a yarn or fabric depends upon the physical and chemical properties of the fiber. The essential physical properties or primary properties are those required for manufacturing or processing the fibers into yarn or fabric. They include a high length-to-width ratio, adequate strength, flexibility, cohesiveness, and uniformity. Many fibrous substances lack one or more essential qualities required of textile fibers. They may not, for example, be sufficiently long to be spun into a yarn. Or they may be too weak, too inflexible, and too thick in diameter to use, or too easily damaged in spinning and weaving. It is, therefore, clear that out of the fibrous substances found in nature, only those that have desirable properties, which have led to their great development as raw materials for the textile industry, have been utilized by man for the manufacture of textiles. Hence the term textile fibers.

(1) Length-to-width ratio

For manufactures to be able to spin a fiber into a yarn or manipulate it to produce a nonwoven fabric, the fiber must be long enough to allow processing and slender enough to be flexible. The relationship between length and width of a fiber is called the length-to-width ration. A minimum ration of 100 is thought to be essential, and most fibers have much higher ratios. Fibers shorter than 1.3cm are seldom used in yarn manufacturing.

(2) Strength

A fiber must posses enough strength to withstand processing by available textile machinery and provide the desired durability in its end use. The strength of a specimen subjected to tension load (as distinct from torsion, compression, and shear loads) is usually reported when fiber properties are compared.

Tensile Strength Any one of a number of different laboratory instruments can be used as apply a tension load to a fiber. Most tension are continued until the fiber breaks. The load at that point is called the breaking load or breaking force. The units for measuring breaking force include pounds, grams, and newtons or millinewtons, abbreviated lbf, gf, N, and mN, respectively.

To compare the breaking strengths of materials of varying sizes, it is necessary to express breaking load in terms of the dimensions of the material being tested. When relatively large material specimens are tested, the comparison may be made based on the cross-sectional area of the unstrained specimen; it is expressed as pound-force per square inch or gram-force per square millimeter. These are units for expressing the tensile strength of materials—that is, the maximum resistance of the material to deformation in a tensile test carried to rupture, expressed in force per unit of cross-sectional area of the unstrained specimen.

Tenacity Individual fiber have very small cross-sectional areas, so with them the conventional units for tensile strength normally are not used. Instead, breaking strength is expressed in terms of the linear density of a material—that is, the mass or weight per unit length. Two common units of fiber linear density are denier (mass in grams of 9000 meters of material) and tex (mass in grams of 1000 meters of material). The tensile stress expressed as force per unit of linear density of the unstrained material is the tenacity, or specific stress, of the material. The units for expressing tenacity include gram-force per denier (g/d or gf/d) and millinewtons per tex(mN/tex).

(3) Flexibility

The ability of a fiber to resist repeated bending or bowing without rupture is flexibility or pliability. Many materials have fibrous forms that would not make practical textile fibers because they lack the flexibility to withstand the repeated bending required in the manufacture of a yarn or fabric.

Flexibility also is important in end-use performance because it influence the hand and draping quality of textiles for apparel and home furnishings and permits fabrics to be creased without rupturing. Industrial fabrics for automobile seat belts and fan belts, which are subjected to repeated bending, also require flexible fibers.

(4) Cohesiveness

With the current methods of yarn formation and direct fiber-to-fabric production, staple fibers must be able to adhere to each other or cling together. This property is known as cohesiveness or spinning quality. The surface contours of fibers directly affect cohesiveness.

Cohesiveness is less important for filament fibers than for staple fibers, because the length of filaments permits them to be twisted together to form yarns. It is important, however, that these filaments do not repel one another.

Cohesiveness of fibers affects yarn fineness and evenness. In turn, such properties as yarn strength, fabric thickness, surface contour, and durability are ultimately affected.

(5) Uniform

Fibers that are similar in length, strength, fineness, cohesiveness, and flexibility, can be processed together with less difficulty than dissimilar fibers. Fibers conforming to the same specifications for these properties are said to exhibit uniformity. One of the positive attributes of manmade fibers is that they can be produced to exact specifications so they will be of the same length, strength, and fineness and accept dyes and finishes evenly. Fibers manufactured in the same production run or lot are virtually identical. Such a lot is usually designated by an identification number, referred to as a merge number, that can be traced to a specific manufacturing facility and a specific batch of chemicals.

Natural fibers, because they are produced under so many different conditions, are more variable. To provide some uniformity, it is necessary to combine or blend fibers from several lots. Today it is common to run laboratory tests to measure fiber properties as an aid to blending fibers in manufacturing processes. A blend of particular length, strength, and fineness may be specified to reduce later problems in processing.

Fiber uniformity also becomes important when manufacturers want to blend different generic fiber groups. Polyester fibers can be produced to be compatible with wool or cotton. When more than two fibers are blended, uniformity becomes even more important.

1.2.2.2 The Secondary Properties of Textile Fibers / 纺织纤维的其他性能

The secondary fiber properties help determined consumer satisfaction with a product influence the selection of specific end use, and affect processing. These include mass, fineness, luster, color, moisture absorption, elongation and recovery, resiliency, thermal properties, and abrasion resistance.

Each textile fiber has its own talents or eccentricities, silk has high luster, wool does not though with markedly superiority in the case of heavier fabrics; cashmere is exceptionally soft and luxurious to the touch; and the color of camel's hair cannot be removed easily. But comparison of fiber qualities and characteristics requires the use of certain basic terms and a technical vocabulary. Definitions of these terms and their meanings covering, in the main, length, fineness or diameter, strength or tenacity, elongation, elasticity or resiliency, cohesion, flexibility, absorbency or moisture content, twist, spinnability, abrasive resistance, and dimensional stability are of importance in textile engineering from the viewpoint of technological processes.

(1) Moisture absorption

Moisture absorption is the ability that a fiber can absorb water from the atmosphere. It may affect apparel comfort, fabric care, textile processing and fiber price. The moisture absorption of a fiber can be expressed as moisture content and moisture regain. Moisture content is the amount of moisture expressed as a percentage of the original or wet weight. Moisture regain is the amount of the moisture expressed as a percentage of the dry weight.

(2) Fineness

Fineness of a fiber is a relative measure of size, diameter, linear density, or mass per unit length expressed in a variety of unit.

Linear density can be expressed in terms of denier and tex. It is the most common method for comparing fiber fineness. Denier is the weight in grams of 9000 meters of a fiber or yarn. Tex is the weight in grams of 1000 meters of a fiber or yarn.

Being the fundamental units used in the making of textile yarns and fabrics, textile fibers contribute to the hand, texture, and appearance of fabrics; they influence and contribute to the performance of fabrics; they determine to a large extent the amount and kind of service required of fabrics; and they have much to do with the cost of fabric. Successfully, textile fibers must be readily available, constant in supply, and inexpensive. They must, of course, have, so far as their properties are concerned, sufficient strength, pliability, length, and cohesiveness to be spun into yarns.

Glossary of Technical Terms / 专业词汇：

polymer	聚合体
flexibility	可弯曲性
cohesiveness	抱合性，内聚性
luster	光泽度
moisture absorption	吸湿性
elastic recovery	弹性回复
thermal properties	热学性能
specimen	试样，样品
tenacity	强度
breaking load	断裂负荷
denier	旦尼尔
pliability	可挠性，柔韧性
flammability	可燃性
hydrophobic	拒水的
moisture content	含水量，含水率
length-to-width ratio	长径比
fineness	细度
uniformity	均匀度，整齐度
color	色彩
elongation	伸长
resiliency	弹性变形；弹力
abrasion resistance	耐磨性
tensile strength	拉伸强力，断裂强力
stress	应力
linear density	线密度
tex	特克斯
extensibility	伸长率
spinning quality	纺纱性能
hydrophilic	亲水的
moisture regain	回潮率

Questions / 思考题：

1. What are the main kinds of textiles described by their end uses?

2. What are the essential properties of textile fibers?
3. How the fiber properties influence the fabric performances?

Activities / 实践作业：

List ten different articles of your own apparel, note from the labels the kinds of fibers from which each are made, and indicate the fiber trademarks, if any.

Chapter Two
Natural Cellulosic Fiber / 天然纤维素纤维

Objectives / 学习目标:

1. Introduce the major varieties of cotton.
2. State the main properties of cotton, flax and ramie fiber.
3. State the microscopic feature of cotton, flax and ramie fiber.

Plant fibers are composed of cellulose, so are classified as cellulosic natural fibers. Natural cellulosic fibers may be produced from seed hairs, plant stems, leaves, or bark. In general, cellulosics provide excellent comfort properties, a high level of durability, and a strong affinity for dyes at a low cost.

Cotton, linen, and ramie are the three important cellulosic fibers.

2.1 Cotton / 棉

Cotton, which comes from seed hairs, is the most widely used of the natural cellulosic fibers and is well known to most consumers. The cotton grows on the plant as long hair attached to the seeds (inside the boll).

2.1.1 Cotton Species / 棉纤维的品种

There are numerous varieties of cotton grown all over the world. Sea Island cotton is the best of the various types of cotton. Such basic characteristics as length and fineness of the cotton fiber are dependent on the type of the seed used. Sea Island cotton [Fig. 2-1 (a)] has a length of 33~46mm, and Upland cotton [Fig. 2-1 (b)] has a shorter length of 23~32mm. Other species of cotton such as African cotton and Indian cotton has a fiber length of 17~24mm, such a short fiber is difficult to be used in spinning processes. However fiber properties are also sensitive to changes in environmental conditions during the growth period. All variety of cotton inherently contains a small percentage of short fibers. But any drastic changes in climatic conditions can result in the unbalance of the normal properties. The proportions of short and immature fibers in a cotton are a major factor in determining its quality and are a source of nuisance during processing.

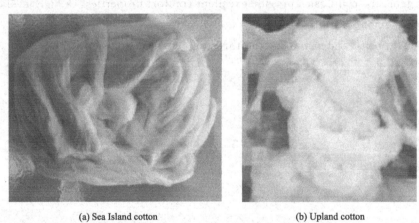

(a) Sea Island cotton   (b) Upland cotton

Fig. 2-1 The main species of cotton

2.1.2 Fiber Production / 棉纤维初加工

Cotton can be picked by hand, by mechanical picking machines, or by stripping devices. After the cotton is picked, it is taken to cotton gin, where the fibers, called cotton lint or ginned cotton by the trade, is separated from the seed. Short fibers left on the seed are called linter. These fibers are too short in length for yarns manufacturing, usually declared waste. There two types of cotton gin, saw-type cotton gin and roll-type cotton gin (Fig. 2-2).

(a) Saw-type cotton gin   (b) Roll-type cotton gin

Fig. 2-2　The two type of cotton gin

Before yarn manufacture, cotton is graded, sorted, and blended to insure uniform yarn quality. Cotton is graded on the basis of its color, staple length, fineness, and freedom from foreign matter. In American, cotton can be divided into seven-step scale from good-middling (best) to good-ordinary (poorest). Good-middling is the whitest, longest, finest, cleanest, and most lustrous of the lot. It requires the least amount of effort to produce high-quality cotton goods. Good-ordinary may be yellowish or gray, contain many bits of twigs and other trash, and is made up of the shortest, coarsest, dullest fibers.

In China, cotton is classified into seven grades according to the maturity, color and luster, ginning quality of the fiber.

2.1.3　Morphology / 形态特征

The cotton fiber may be from 0.3 to 5.5cm long. Under the microscope it appears as a ribbonlike structure that is twisted at irregular intervals along its length (Fig. 2-3). The twists, called "convolutions", increase the fiber-to-fiber friction necessary to secure a strong spun yarn. The fiber ranges in color from a yellowish to pure white, and may be very lustrous. However, most cotton is dull.

The cross-section of cotton fiber is kidney-shaped with a central hollow core known as the lumen (Fig. 2-3). The lumen provides a channel for nutrients while the plant is growing. The fiber is found to consist of an outer shell, or cuticle, which surrounds the primary wall. The primary wall, in turn, covers the secondary wall surrounding the lumen. Immature fibers exhibit thin wall structures and larger lumen, where mature fibers have thick walls and a small lumen that may not be continuous.

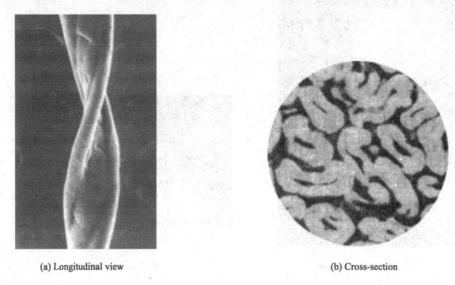

(a) Longitudinal view　　　　　　　　(b) Cross-section

Fig. 2-3　Photomicrograph of cotton fiber

2.1.4　Fiber Properties / 纤维性能

(1) Chemical properties

Cotton fibers are highly resistant to alkalies, but can be damaged by acids. Sodium hydroxide is used to mercerize cotton, and improve some of the fiber properties. The mercerized fibers appear smooth and round when compared with untreated fibers, so exhibit luster.

(2) Tensile properties

Cotton has a moderate tenacity of 26.5~44.1cN/tex. When wet, cotton fiber increases in strength, so it may have a wet strength equal to 110 to 120 percent of the dry strength. This means that fiber care and wet processing techniques do not require modification to compensate for reduced fiber strength when wet.

Cotton has an elongation of 6~9 percent at the breaking point. It is as high as 10 percent of slack mercerized fibers. It has low resiliency, with a recovery of only 75 percent at 2 percent extension.

(3) Moisture absorption

A relatively high level of moisture absorption and good wicking properties help make cotton one of the more comfortable fibers. Because of the hydroxyl groups in the cellulose, cotton has a high attraction for water. As water enters the fiber, cotton swells and its cross-section becomes more rounded. The moisture regain of cotton fiber at standard conditions is 8.5%. At 95% relative humidity, the regain is approximately 15%, and at 100% relative humidity, it may be 25%~27%.

Mercerized cotton fibers have been swollen and can absorb more moisture than non-mercerized fibers. The standard regain of mercerized cotton varies from 8.5% to 10.3%; the latter figure is considered the more common.

(4) Maturity

Maturity of a cotton is characterized by the degree of the development of the cell wall. If a cotton has a well developed wall thickness, it is said to be mature; on the other hand, a cotton fiber with a thin and poorly developed cell wall is said to be immature.

Maturity can be expressed as mature ratio M, percent maturity PM, maturity coefficient M and Micronaire reading M_{ic}.

2.1.5 Uses / 用途

Perhaps more than any other fiber, cotton satisfies the requirements of apparel, home furnishings and industrial uses. It provides fabrics that are strong, lightweight, pliable, easily dyed, and readily laundered. In apparel, cotton provides garments that are comfortable, readily dyed in bright, long-lasting colors, and easy to care for. The major drawbacks are a propensity for cotton yarns to shrink and for cotton cloth to wrinkle. Shrinkage may be controlled by the application of shrink-resistant finishes. Durable-press properties may be imparted by chemical treatment or by blending cotton with more wrinkle-resistant fibers, such as polyester.

In home furnishings, cotton serves in durable, general-service fabrics. Although they may lack the formal appearance of materials made from other fibers, cotton goods provide a comfortable, homey environment. Cotton fabrics have been the mainstay of bed linens and towels for decades, because they are comfortable, durable, and moisture-absorbent. Polyester/cotton blends provide the modern consumer with no-iron sheets and pillowcases that retain a crisp, fresh feel.

Cotton cord, twine, and ropes are used in industry to bind, hold, and lash all kinds of things, from bales to boats. Cotton yarns are used to reinforce belts on drive motors, as cargo nets, and in work clothing.

2.2 Bast Fiber / 韧皮纤维

As the name implies, these fibers are obtained from the inner bark of the stems of plants. The most important fibers in this group are linen (flax), jute, ramie, hemp, and sunn. These fibers are also composed of cellulose. They are made of long, thick-walled cells glued together by noncellulosic materials (lignin and pectin) resulting in long fiber bundles running the entire length of the stem. The amount of noncellulosic material varies considerably from one type of fiber to the other. For example, jute may contain as much as 20% lignin, compared to 8% in flax.

The bast fibers are removed from woody stems by the process known as "retting". The function of this process is to ferment the noncellulosic material binding the fibers and remove it by washing in water. However, the individual fibers, which are extremely short, are not completely separated from one another, but are extracted in strands to make them viable for textile processing.

2.2.1　Flax / 亚麻

Flax was probably the first plant fiber used, and it may be the first fiber from any source used in the Western World. Flax strands are generally processed in lengths varying from 18in up to approximately 36in. This length suffers a loss by the time the strands reach the spinning process. Flax is generally graded on the basis of its color, which is usually yellowish white, but may change depending on the conditions during the process of retting.

2.2.1.1　Morphology / 形态特征

Individual flax fibers vary in length from 0.25 to 2.5in, and are about $25\mu m$ in diameter. The fiber is long, transparent, cylindrical, and has a smooth but sometimes striated appearance. It has a narrow lumen running through the center. In cross section, the cell walls appear thick and polygonal in shape (Fig. 2-4).

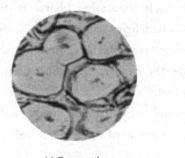
(a) Cross-section

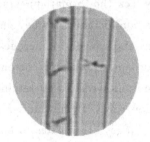
(b) Longitudinal view

Fig. 2-4　Photomicrograph of flax fiber

2.2.1.2　Properties and End Uses / 纤维性能及最终用途

Flax fiber is comparatively stronger than cotton but has very low extensibility. It has an average tenacity of about 60g/tex and approximately 1.8% extension-to-break. It has a regain of about 12% and is about 20% stronger wet than dry. Linen is mainly used in the manufacture of sail cloth, tent fabric, sewing threads, fishing lines, tablecloths, and sheets.

2.2.2　Ramie / 苎麻

Ramie, or China grass, is a bast fiber that has cultivated for hundreds of years in China, the Malay Peninsula, and the Philippine Islands. Now it is being grown in Florida and the West India as well.

2.2.2.1　Morphology / 形态特征

Ramie fibers are long and very fine. It is the only type of bast fiber that can use individual fibers for spinning. From the longitudinal view, ramie fibers have cylindrical, smooth but sometimes striated appearance with joints and cracks on the surface. The cross-section is kidney shape with lumen in the center (Fig. 2-5).

(a) Cross-section　　　　　　　　(b) Longitudinal view

Fig. 2-5　Photomicrograph of ramie fiber

2.2.2.2　Properties / 纤维性能

They are similar to flax in most properties. The fiber is very strong; its tenacity is 46.4 to 65.3cN/tex, and it increases in strength when wet. Ramie fibers are a bit stiffer and more crystalline. For many years, the only ramie seen in the United States was that used as a substitute for flax in table linens. Ramie suddenly began to appear in apparel fabrics during the 1980s, when some of the Asia countries began to blend it with other fibers in an attempt to raise their textile exports. Most of it appears in blends with cotton, rayon, polyester, acrylic, and silk. The fiber is often blended with two or more other fibers.

2.2.3　Jute / 黄麻

Jute is one of the most important fibers used for industrial applications. It is mostly used in making "sack cloth" and carpet-backing fabric. It is primarily grown in India, Pakistan, and to a certain extracted from the China. It is extracted by a retting process similar to the one used for flax. Jute is graded on the basis of its color and string length. Its color varies from yellow to brown to dirty gray, and it is lustrous in appearance. Jute fibers generally have a rough feel; however, the best quality fibers are smooth and soft. The strand length varies from approximately 5 to 12ft. Jute fibers vary greatly in strength and are not as strong as flax or hemp. They have an elongation-to-break of approximately 1.7%. Jute is highly hygroscopic in nature. Besides having many industrial applications, finer quality jute fibers are utilized in furnishing and curtain fabrics. Bleached jute is sometimes blended with wool to provide cheap woven apparel fabrics.

2.2.4　Hemp / 大麻

Hemp comes from the bark of the plant Cannabis Sativa. It is grown in almost all the countries of Europe, and in many parties of Asia. Hemp fiber is extracted from the woody matter by retting and subsequent breaking and scutching. It is coarser than flax and has a dark color. However, the strand length varies from 4 to 10ft. The fiber shows joints and cracks on the surface. It has a tenacity of 5.8 to 6.8 g/d, and both elongation and elasticity are low. Moisture regain at standard conditions is 12 percent, and saturation regain is 30 percent. Hemp is primarily used in making ropes and twines and is woven into fabrics used for sack cloth and canvas.

Glossary of Technical Terms / 专业词汇：

seed hair	籽纤维，种子纤维
gin	轧棉机
linter	棉短绒
mercerize	丝光处理
Sea Island cotton	海岛棉
mercerization	丝光作用
primary wall	初生层
maturity	成熟度
staple length	手扯长度
noncellulosic material	非纤维素物质
retting	沤麻
stiff	硬挺
jute	黄麻
bast fiber	韧皮纤维
cotton lint	皮棉
trash	杂质
mercerized cotton	丝光棉
uplands cotton	陆地棉

lumen	中腔，腔管
second wall	次生层
convolution	转曲
lignin	木质素
pectin	果胶
scutching	打麻
stiffness	硬挺度
ramie	苎麻

Questions / 思考题：

1. What are the major factors in determining the quality of cotton fiber?
2. Sketch the cross-section of the cotton fiber and linen fiber, and label their parts.
3. Explain why cellulsic fibers have a relatively high moisture regain.

Activities / 实践作业：

Look at items in stores and catalogs to see what cellulosic fibers are being used for various end uses. What blend levels are being used, and what combinations of fibers? What kind of care instructions are provide for these fabrics?

Chapter Three
Natural Protein Fibers / 天然蛋白质纤维

Objectives / 学习目标：

1. To list and describe the properties of the two major protein fibers, and familiar with some specialty hair fibers.
2. To identify the differences between wool and silk.
3. To identify the legislation that applies to wool and silk.

The protein fibers are naturally occurring animal products. The two major protein fibers are wool and silk. Wool is the fiber from the fleece of a sheep or lamb or the hair of a fur-bearing animal; silk is the fiber extruded by the silkworm, in the form of a cocoon, for protection in its pupa stage. Spider silk, which is extruded by the spider to form a web, sometimes is classified as a textile fiber.

Less than 5 percent of the fibers consumed in the United States are protein fibers, but their unique properties make them an important object of study in textile science. Of the two, wool fibers are the more widely used; they provide warmth, a pleasant hand, attractive appearance, good absorbency, and resiliency. Silk, noted for its lustrous appearance and unique hand, has always been considered a luxury fiber.

3.1 Wool / 羊毛

The major source of the world's wool is Australia. Russia is the second in production, and New Zealand is third. China is producing a major quantity of the carpet-grade fiber. Several breeds of sheep are raised for their fiber. Wool from the Merino sheep is very fine wool. The Merino fiber has a small diameter and is the standard against which other fibers are judged.

3.1.1 Morphology / 形态特征

The wool fiber has a spirally crimped form. Under microscope, it generally appears as a circular cylinder with scales on the surface (Fig. 3-1). The cross-section is nearly circular (Fig. 3-1). Wool fiber is made up of different layers. The outer layer, which contains the scales, is called the epidermis or cuticle. The cortical cells, or cortex, just under the cuticle make up about 90 percent of the fiber mass and consist of fibrils. There are two types of cortical cells, referred to as ortho-and para-cortical cells; the crimp, or curl, in wool fibers is controlled by their differences. The central canal, or medulla, of the fiber, which may not be visible in photographs, allows nutrients to reach the fiber during its growth phase and contains the pigment that gives fibers their color.

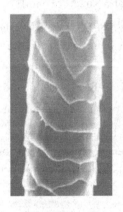
(a) Longitudinal view

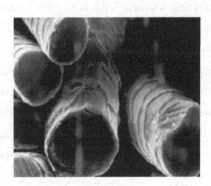
(b) Cross-section

Fig. 3-1　Photomicrograph of wool fiber

3.1.2 Properties of Wool Fiber / 羊毛纤维的性能

Most wool fibers have a white or creamy color, although some breeds of sheep yield brown or black wool. Wool fiber has a natural luster depending on the type of wool. Merino wool are generally Semidull, where-as some other varieties have a silky luster. Wool fiber has a density of 1.32, which makes it slightly lighter than cotton. Wool and other protein fibers with folded molecules are characterized by low tenacity but higher extensibility. Wool and other hair fibers are not very good under high stresses, but show large recovery from high strains. This makes the wool fibers highly resilient. In other words, wool fibers have a tendency to return completely to their original shape after small deformations, which is a great asset in apparel fabrics.

Wool has an equilibrium moisture regain of 13%~19% depending on the form and condition. When a fiber absorbs moisture, heat is liberated. This liberation of heat has physiologic consequences. The high moisture regain properties of wool also contribute partly toward its non-flammability characteristics. Felting shrinkage is an irreversible reaction that occurs when moisture, heat, and pressure are applied to the fiber. The scales on one fiber tend to interlock with contiguous fibers, so the fibers become entangled and matted. Wool is fairly resistant to mild acids, but it is particularly sensitive to various industrial chemical modification treatments by which wool fabrics can be made shrink and felt proof.

The natural crimp in wool is of great importance, since it results in making a yarn fluffy, thereby trapping air in the interstices between the fibers. This trapping of air helps in forming an insulating layer, thus imparting the characteristic of warmth.

3.1.3 End Uses of Wool Fiber / 羊毛纤维的应用

Wool is used primarily in apparel and home furnishings. Wool fabrics are naturally crease-resistant, flexible, elastic, absorbent, and warm. The performance of wool in terms of resiliency and thermal protection in floor coverings and winter apparel traditionally has been the standard against which other fibers are measured. The International Wool Secretariat (IWS) is an international organization formed to play the role of a central research and development group for the wool industry and to promote the use of wool fiber. The Wool Bureau in the United States is a branch of the IWS. The international Woolmark and Woolblend symbols are licensed in the United States by the Wool Bureau. Products displaying these symbols must meet certain performance specifications set by the Wool Bureau. The Woolmark is used for products containing 100 percent wool; the Woolblend Mark is a symbol used for products containing at least 60 percent wool (Fig. 3-2). Wool fabrics are used primarily in cold weather clothing. Household uses for wool include blankets, rugs, carpets, and upholstery fabrics. The two major types of wool fabrics are woolens and worsteds. The terms are derived from their respective methods of yarn manufacturing. Woolen fabrics usually have a soft hand and a low bulk density. They are usually rougher, coarser, and thicker than worsted fabrics, which usually have a smooth and crisp hand.

(a) Pure wool   (b) Wool blend

Fig. 3-2 International symbols of wool.

3.2 Specialty Animal Fibers / 特种动物毛

Hair and wool fibers from animals other than sheep are usually referred to as specialty hair fibers. These products of the goat and camel families are by no means inferior to wool, nor are they limited in their uses. The term "specialty" arose because of their scarcity.

Cashmere: The fine down (wool) that grows under the coarse outer hair of the Kashmir goat (Fig. 3-3) is known as cashmere. China and India produce most of the commercial fiber. The down is combed from the animal in the spring and summer, and yields are estimated to be about 250g per animal. Such a small yield can only be justified by a superior quality of fiber.

Cashmere wool fibers are between 2 and 10cm long, may be white, pale brown, or gray, and somewhat finer than sheep's wool. The tenacity, stretch, and elasticity are essentially the same as for ordinary wool, but because of its smaller diameter, cashmere is much softer (Fig. 3-4). Used exclusively in apparel, this luxury fiber makes fabrics that are soft, warm, and lustrous, and have excellent drape.

Mohair: While the sheep has been bred to maximize wool production, the Angora goat (Fig. 3-5) has been bred for its long, lustrous hair, called mohair. Before the Industrial Revolution, mohair was almost exclusively obtained from Turkey. However, introduction of the Angora goat into Texas and California near the end of the nineteenth century led to a thriving industry. Today the United States is the major producer and user of mohair.

Mohair is very similar in physical and chemical structure to wool. Fibers rang from 10 to 30cm in length, are covered by scales, and possess a natural crimp. The scales on mohair are flatter than those on wool, so that the fiber has a smoother hand (Fig. 3-6). In addition, mohair is finer than most wools, and more tightly curled. It is equivalent to wool in strength, elasticity, and dyeability.

Fig. 3-3 Kashmir goat

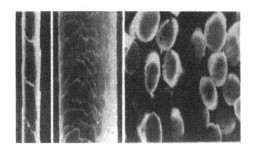

Fig. 3-4 The morphology of cashmere

Fig. 3-5 Angora goat

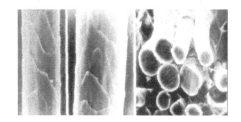

Fig. 3-6 The morphology of mohair

Mohair is exceptionally resistant to abrasion and is very durable. Its tight curl provides interesting esthetics in complex fabric constructions. The major uses include sweaters, suits, and upholstery. It is often blended with wool.

Camel Hair: The family Camelidae, along with goats, is the other major source of specialty hair fiber. This small family of animals has two branches, the Old Word camel and the llama (Fig. 3-7). The camel branch is composed of the dromedary (one-humped) and the bactrian (two-humped), while the llama branch comprises the alpaca, guanaco, haurizo, llama, misti, and vicuna. Of these, the bactrian camel, alpaca, and vicuna are the most important to the textile industry.

The bactrian camel of Central Asia is the major source of camel hair. The hair that is used in textiles is the fine undercoat of the camel, which is shed during the spring and summer. It ranges in color from pale reddish-brown to dark brown and black. The fibers, about the same diameter as wool, range in length from 2 to 12cm, and are covered with scales (Fig. 3-8). The camel hair scales are not as well defined as those of wool, so the fibers do not felt as readily. Its major use is in men's outerwear, particularly overcoats. Garments of camel hair are warm, durable, relatively lightweight, and comfortable.

Fig. 3-7 Camel

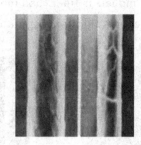
Fig. 3-8 The morphology of camel hair

Alpaca: In the high Andean Mountain regions of northern South America, the Indian tribes have made use of the llama family as beasts of burden for centuries. The alpaca, however, has been bred mainly for its fleece. These small animals, which stand about 1meter high, produce a beautiful, fine, strong, and durable fiber.

Alpaca wool is sheared from the animal every other year, to yield 2 to 3kg of fiber. The fibers may be from 20 to 30 long, and range in color from black through gray and brown to white. Cloth prepared from alpaca is soft, warm, glossy in appearance, and yields interesting color variations without the use of dyestuffs. It is often found in suits, dresses, upholstery, and garment linings.

Vicuna: The finest, softest, and rarest of the wool fibers is that obtained from the vicuna. This mammal, about the size of a very large dog, roams the Peruvian mountains at elevations of 4,000meters or more. Attempts to domesticate the vicuna have so far proved economically unsuccessful, and the animal is hunted under government license. One animal yields about 1/2kg of fleece.

Vicuna wool is about half the diameter of sheep's wool. It is extremely soft, yet stronger than other wools and hair of equal fineness. It ranges in color from pale cinnamon to pure white. The scales of fiber are very fine, giving a smooth hand to the yarn, and reducing its propensity to felt. Vicuna ranks among the most luxurious and expensive fibers. Used chiefly in suits and overcoats, vicuna garments are noted for warmth, softness, and light weight. The cloth is relatively weak, however, and must be handled carefully.

3.3 Silk / 蚕丝

From its discovery, in about 2650 B.C., until today, silk has been known as the "queen of the fibers". Japan and China are the word's major sources of silk, although minor quantities come from India, Italy, and Korea.

Silk is a natural protein secreted by the larvae of several different moths. The two main categories are cultivated silk and wild silk or tussah. Cultivated silk is more lustrous and lighter in color than tussah. The luster of the fiber is affected by cross-sectional shape.

3.3.1 Fiber Production / 制丝

To obtain silk, workers stifle the larvae and boil the cocoons in a carefully controlled bath to loosen the sericin coating. The end of the filament is brushed off the cocoon and, along with ends from one or two other cocoons, unwound. This process is known as reeling (Fig. 3-9). The filaments are usually twisted to form a silk yarn of about 6 to 8 denier. The raw silk may now be used as is. However, it is generally thrown, or twisted, with two or three other yarns to form a heavier cord. This cord is what is used in cloth manufacture.

Fig. 3-9   Reeling process

The sericin coating is generally removed after the yarn has been woven or knitted into cloth by a process known as degumming, in which the natural sericin is removed in hot, soapy water. Degummed, or soft silks are softer and more lustrous than the hard silk, which still retains its sericin coat.

3.3.2 Morphology / 形态特征

Under the microscope, raw silk is found to consist of a pair of fine filaments bonded by sericin gum. The bave, as the dual strand is called, is elliptical in cross-section. A longitudinal view reveals a rough, cracked surface containing many striations (Fig. 3-10). The roughness is in the sericin layer. When degummed, the individual strands, or brins, are revealed as triangles with rounded points.

3.3.3 Properties / 纤维性能

Cultivated silk is off-white to cream in color; and tussah silk is more likely to be

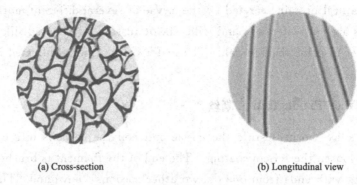

(a) Cross-section   (b) Longitudinal view

Fig. 3-10 Photomicrograph of silk

tan to medium brown. Silk is one of the strongest natural fibers. Its dry tenacity is between 2.4 and 5.1g/d. It loses 15 to 20 percent strength when wet. The elongation at break of dry fibers is between 10 and 25 percent. Silk has average resiliency. Wrinkles and creases do not hang out as quickly or completely as in wool, because the silk fiber does not contain the cystine linkages of wool. The standard moisture regain of silk is 11percent. It is not quite as absorbent as wool but is more absorbent than other fibers. High absorbency makes the fiber comfortable to wear and easy to dye.

3.3.4 End Uses of Silk / 蚕丝的应用

Silk is used for luxury apparel, household textiles, and medical sutures. It is popular in men's neckties for its hand and drape. Silk apparel fabrics are available in a wide range of weights and constructions. The fiber is used alone and in blends with other fibers. Silk blends are usually made with spun yarns.

Glossary of Technical Terms / 专业词汇：

Merino sheep	美利奴绵羊
cortex	皮质
para-cortical	偏皮质
pigment	色素
crease	折皱
crease resistance	抗皱性
dimensional stability	尺寸稳定性
felting shrinkage	毡缩性，缩绒性
silky luster	丝光
non-flammability	阻燃性
woolen	粗梳毛织物
washable wool fabric	可机洗羊毛
Woolmark	纯羊毛标志

Wool Bureau	羊毛局
fibroin	丝蛋白，丝
reeling	缫丝
degumming	脱胶
weighted silk	重磅真丝
raw silk	生丝
International Wool Secretariat	(IWS)国际羊毛局
epidermis/cuticle	表皮
cortical cell	皮层细胞
ortho-cortical	正皮质(层)，正外皮
medulla	毛髓
fibril	原纤维
hygroscopic	吸湿的
outerwear	外衣，外套
felting	毡合
semidull	半消光
modification treatment	改性处理
thermal protection	保暖性
worsted	精纺毛织物
shrink resistant finish	防缩整理
Woolblend symbol	混纺羊毛标志
cultivated silk	家蚕丝
sericin	丝胶
throwing	捻丝
bave	茧丝
brin	单丝，丝素
degummed silk	熟丝

Questions / 思考题：

1. When viewed through the microscope, what can you see from the cross-section of a wool fiber?

2. What are the properties of silk and wool that make them attractive to consumers?

Activities / 实践作业：

What animal fibers are present in most of your own clothing? What blend levels are being used, and what combinations of fibers? What kind of care instructions are provide for these fabrics?

Chapter Four
Manufactured Cellulosic Fibers / 再生纤维素纤维

Objectives / 学习目标：

1. Introduce the main types of manufactured cellulosic fibers.
2. Compare the differences between the three types of viscose rayon.
3. State the main characteristics of Tencel.

The first manmade, or manufactured fibers were produced from plant materials in an attempt to duplicate the product of a silkworm eating mulberry leaves. The silkworm feeds on a cellulosic product, but the fiber it secretes is protein. The manufactured fibers produced via chemical digestion of cellulose are regenerated cellulose, or cellulose acetate. Today, three cellulosic fibers, with quite different properties, are defined by the TFPIA. They are rayon and acetate.

Rayon—a manufactured fiber composed of regenerated cellulose, as well as manufactured fibers composed of regenerated cellulose in which substituents have replaced not more than 15% of the hydrogen of the hydroxyl groups.

Acetate—a manufactured fiber in which the fiber-forming substance is cellulose acetate. Where not less than 92% of the hydroxyl groups are acetylated, the term triacetate may be used as generic description of the fiber.

4.1 Rayon / 黏胶纤维

There two basic types of rayon were developed by using different chemicals and manufacturing techniques. They are viscose rayon and cuprammonium rayon. Viscose rayon are the most widely used type. Cuprammonium rayon is made by a process that is much simpler than that for viscose. The major end uses of cuprammonium rayon are linings and lightweight dresses.

Viscose rayon have three major types. They are regular rayon, high-tenacity rayon, and high-wet-modulus (HWM) rayon. Modal is a trademarked HWM fiber from an Austrian textile company, Lenzing. High-tenacity rayon is produced by applying additional stretch during drawing (in hot aqueous acid). The purpose of stretch is to increase the degree of alignment of cellulose molecules along the fiber axis, and in addition, cause an increase in the proportion of "skin to core".

4.1.1 Morphology / 形态特征

From longitudinal view, regular viscose rayon has uniform diameter and striations. The cross-section of fiber is quite irregular serrated shape, and has "skin and core" structure.

High-tenacity rayon has less irregular contour in cross section, so show fewer striations in the longitudinal view. High wet-modulus rayon may appear neatly round cross section and smooth surface in the longitudinal view.

Cuprammonium rayon has a round or oval shape in cross section. In longitudinal view, it is uniform in width, and has smooth surface with no striation.

Fig. 4-1 display the cross-section shapes of the major manmade cellulosic fibers.

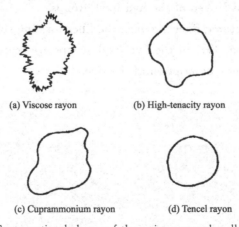

(a) Viscose rayon (b) High-tenacity rayon

(c) Cuprammonium rayon (d) Tencel rayon

Fig. 4-1 Cross-sectional shapes of the major manmade cellulosic fibers

4.1.2 Properties / 纤维性能

Viscose rayon is a medium-weight fiber with fair to good strength and abrasion resistance. It loses 30% to 50% of its strength when wet, high-tenacity rayon and high-weight modulus rayon may lose less strength than regular rayon. And the fiber recovers strength when dry. So the fabric may require great caution in laundering, and is dry cleanable. It has very poor elasticity, so the fabric wrinkle easily. The moisture regain of viscose rayon is about 11%, so the fabric is comfortable to wear. There are no static or pilling problems.

4.1.3 End Uses / 最终用途

Rayon is widely used in apparel, home furnishings, and industrial applications, such as dresses, shirts, draperies, medical products, nonwoven fabrics etc. Today, rayon is one of the least expensive fibers. Blending rayon with other, less hydrophilic fibers such as polyester and nylon, yields fabrics that are softer, more comfortable, and inexpensive. Rayon filament, used in combination with spun yarns of other fibers, gives strength to the fabric without sacrificing comfort.

Cuprammonium rayon is most often used in high-quality women's undergarments and dresses linings.

4.2 Acetate / 醋酯纤维

Cellulose acetate was discovered in 1869, but it was 35 years later that Henry and Camille Dreyfus developed an economical process for its commercial manufacture. The production of this fiber began in England in 1921, and in the U.S. in 1924. For many years the public thought of both cellulose acetate and regenerated cellulose fibers as the same material, "artificial silk". In 1951, however, the Federal Trade Commission ruled that rayon meant regenerated cellulose, and that acetate meant cellulose acetate.

There are two types of cellulose acetate fibers, triacetate and acetate (some times called diacetate).

4.2.1 Morphology / 形态特征

Acetate fibers are somewhat irregular in cross section, with a shape more similar to some high-tenacity rayon than to regular viscose. It is often difficult to distinguish acetate and rayon fibers by cross-sectional views.

In longitudinal view, fibers with irregular cross sections appear to have striations along the fiber length, which are visible because light is reflected in an irregular pattern off the surface of the fiber.

4.2.2 Properties / 纤维性能

The properties of acetate and rayon fibers are quite different. Acetate is a heat-sensitive fiber and may be considered similar to true thermoplastic fibers in many of its properties, whereas rayon is more similar to the natural cellulosic fibers. Triacetate softens at a higher temperature than acetate and can be given a heat-set in garment manufacture, using carefully controlled presses. Both acetate and triacetate resist wrinkling better than cotton. Wrinkles hang out if the garments are properly stored after wearing.

Both acetate and triacetate are weaker than cotton owing to lower crystallinity and reduced hydrogen bonding. The abrasion resistance is poor for the same reasons. The fabrics have excellent drape and luxurious hand.

In general, relatively amorphous fibers absorb more moisture than more crystalline fibers. The presence of hydroxyl groups increase moisture absorbency. Rayon absorbs more moisture than acetate, and diacetate absorbs more moisture than triacetate. At standard condition, the moisture regain of regular viscose rayon is 13%; of acetate, 6.5%; and of triacetate, about 3.2%.

4.2.3 End uses / 最终用途

Both acetate and triacetate are widely used in apparel and home furnishings. In apparel, both fibers are suitable for a wide range of fabrics. They have good drape, fair wrinkle resistance, and a pleasing luster. In blends with rayon, they provide improved wrinkle resistance and a pleasing luster, and resist absorbing water-borne stains. When blended with wool, they reduce the tendency to shrink and felt. However, decreased and durability may result.

4.3 A New Type of Manufactured Cellulosic Fiber-Lyocell / 新型再生纤维素纤维——莱赛尔纤维

In 1989, Courtaulds introduced a solvent-spun cellulosic fiber, for which they use an amine oxide called NMMO, an organic solvent that is much less harmful than others used in fiber production. Wood pulp is dissolved in hot amine oxide to produce a clear, viscous solution, which is filtered and extruded into a bath of dilute NMMO, where the fiber coagulates as reconstituted cellulose. The fibers are washed and dried, and the solvent is recovered for further use. Because the cellulose is not regenerated, the fiber has a molecular structure different from that of viscose. Since this is a close-loop system, and virtually all solvent can be recovered and used again, the process is largely pollution-free. The first commercial production is in 1992, with the trademark of Tencel.

4.3.1 Morphology / 形态特征

Lyocell has a smooth surface and a round cross section quite different from those of viscose rayon.

4.3.2 Properties / 纤维性能

Lyocell has a dry strength comparable to cotton and some polyester, very high wet-modulus, and it retains 85% of its dry strength when wet. Being made up of cellulose, the fiber has good moisture absorbency, the moisture regain at standard condition is 11.5%. The fabric has good static resistance, cool hand, and good heat resistance.

Lyocell fibers have a tendency to fibrillation—to splitting off if abraded when wet, forming surface fibrils. This gives a very soft "peach skin" hand, then the fabrics show a unique appearance. But the tendency of fibrillation can also result in a difference in light reflection from the surface that may be interpreted as graying. Therefore, a non-fibrillation variation is developed—Tencel A100 (by Acordis), and Lyocell LF (by Lenzing).

Because acetate fibers have fewer associative forces between the molecular chains than rayon fibers, acetate fibers generally have lower tenacities. The manufactured cellulosic fibers tend to lose strength when wet. The high-wet-modulus fibers do not lose as much strength as regular rayon.

Glossary of Technical Terms / 专业词汇：

cellulose acetate	纤维素醋酸酯
high tenacity rayon	高强黏纤
high-wet-modulus rayon	高湿模量黏纤
solvent spinning	溶液纺丝
cuprammonium	铜氨纤维
pollution-free	无污染
crystallinity	结晶度
hydroxyl group	羟基
regular rayon	普通黏纤
melting spinning	熔融纺丝
fibrillation	原纤化
peach skin	桃皮绒

orientation 取向度

Questions / 思考题：

1. Describe the differences among the three major types of rayon.
2. What is Tencel?
3. In what end uses can you find rayon and acetate products?
4. Both rayon and cotton are made of cellulose. Compare their performance properties and explain the differences.

Activities / 实践作业：

Survey the labels on garments and upholstery fabric containing manufactured cellulose fibers. What fibers are present, and in what percentages?

Chapter Five
Synthetic Fibers / 合成纤维

Objectives / 学习目标：

1. State the main properties and end uses of nylon.
2. Describe the characteristics of polyester fibers.
3. Describe the main properties and end uses of aramid fiber.
4. State the end uses of spandex.

5.1 Polyamide Fibers / 聚酰胺纤维

Synthetic polyamide fibers, generally known as nylon, were the first successful commercially produced synthetic fibers. They were developed in 1938 by DuPont. The word Nylon was coined at DuPont, supposedly as a derivative of the rumored no-run properties of stocking made from the material. Today they constitute a major part of the fiber production in the textile industry.

Polyamide molecules are obtained by the condensation polymerization of long-chain molecules such as a diamine with dicarboxylic acid, or self-condensation of amine acid or its derivative such as a lactam. The general processes for nylon production consists of polymerization, melting spinning, and drawing. There are a number of experimentally produced synthetic polyamide fibers, but the two most important commercial ones that form the bulk of world production are nylon 66 and nylon 6.

Nylon fibers have high strength, good elasticity, and a high level of abrasion resistance. The tenacity of Nylon is about 4.5~5.8g/den, and the elongation is 30% at break. It is only about 10% weaker when wet. Nylon fibers have 100% elastic recovery at 4% extension. These properties make them used for reinforcement in the heel of socks and in other garments subject to severe abrasion to prolong the useful life of the garments. Even though nylon 66 and nylon 6 do not differ in basic chemical structure, there are certain subtle differences in the physical characteristics of the two types of fibers.

Nylon (both types) fibers are produced in a multiplicity of finenesses (deniers) and staple lengths. They are produced as multifilament yarns, monofilament, and tow in bright, semidull, and dull luster. In addition to the circular cross section, some manufacturers make nylon fibers in trilobal and multilobal cross-sectional forms. Nylon is thermoplastic in nature and possesses heat-setting characteristics. It is available in crimped and various textured (bulked) forms.

It has a moisture regain of 4%~4.5% at standard conditions [(72±2) °F and 65% R.H.]. It is not affected by most chemicals, but concentrated hydrochloric and sulfuric acids tend to deteriorate the fiber and cause loss of strength. Also, prolonged exposure to light or ultraviolet light can cause deterioration in fiber tensile properties. Nylon fibers melt when heated to high temperatures. As a result, when nylon fabric ignites, the molten polymer falls away and thus inhibits flame propagation. Nylon has very good dyeing characteristics and may be dyed with range of dyestuffs.

Nylon fibers and filaments are used in a number of textile applications because of their outstanding mechanical properties, excellent recovery, and high resistance to abrasion and wear. In addition to apparel and house-hold textile applications, they are extensively used in carpets and industrial applications such as tire yarns, hose, parachutes, belting and filter fabrics to name a few.

5.2 Polyester Fibers / 聚酯纤维

Imperial Chemical Industries (ICI) purchase the British patent rights for the fiber and began manufacturing Terylene in England, DuPont purchase the U.S. patent application from C. P. A., Ltd., and eventually received U. S. Patent 2,465,319; which allowed them to produce a fiber in the United States. The Du Pont fiber, was introduced to the American press in 1951 as Dacron; commercial production of the fiber started at the Kinston, North Carolina, plant in 1953. In 1958, Eastman Chemical Pro ducts, a division of Tennessee Eastman, introduced its new polyester fiber, Kodel. The fiber was produced by a different from that for Terylene and Dacron. Full-scale production of the fiber was not begun until 1960.

Polyester fibers form the largest group of fibers that are used to satisfy the demands of the textile industry, polyester polymers are produced by a condensation reaction, and the linkages between the monomers are produced by the formation of ester groups. There are a number of different types of polyester polymers, but the two most important used in the production of textile fibers are (1) polyethylene terephthalate fibers (PET polyester fibers, e. g., Dacron) and (2) poly-1, 4-cyclohexylene-dimethylene terephthalate fiber (PCDT polyester fiber, e. g., Kodel).

Polyester fibers have a smooth surface and generally have a circular cross section, except for some special types produced in trilobal form.

Polyester is produced in a wide range of deniers and staple with bright, semidull, or dull luster. It has excellent tensile properties. The tenacity of fibers ranges from 2.5 to 9.5 grams per denier. Fibers with tenacities of 22 to 30 cN/tex are used almost exclusivity for apparel. Elongation varies with the types of fiber and ranges from about 10 to 60 percent. In general, fibers with high tenacity have low elongation, and low-strength fibers are higher elongation. Elasticity recovery of polyester fibers is very good. Most of the high-tenacity polyesters exhibit 100% recovery after 2% elongation. Polyester fibers have a very low moisture regain of 0.4% at standard conditions. The low moisture pickup of the fibers makes them quick-dry, hag and at times difficult to process. Low moisture levels are also associated with a buildup of static electricity. It has a relatively high coefficient of friction and smooth surface. It is a thermoplastic fiber and melts when heated to high temperatures. It fuses and forms a hard bead when ignited. In all practical senses, polyester fiber is an inert fiber, highly resistant to most of the common organic solvents. Polyester fibers are hydrophobic in character. They are therefore dyed by dyestuffs, such as disperse dyes, and so on, which are insoluble in water.

Polyester fiber or fabric may be heat set to impart dimensional stability which may be affected by any subsequent heat treatments or finishing processes. Polyester filament yarns may be texturized to produce bulk and stretch characteristics in woven or knitted fabrics.

Polyester fibers are used in many textile applications including carpets, upholstery, and industrial uses. A very large proportion are produced in staple form, which is used in blends with wool, cotton, viscose, rayon, and linen. The inclusion of polyester fibers in blends improves the wear and abrasion resistance and the "ease of care" characteristics of fabrics. Other areas of polyester fiber use include fillings in pillows and quilts. Sewing thread, tire yarns, conveyor belts, and ropes and twines.

5.3 Polyacrylic Fibers / 聚丙烯腈纤维

Polyacrylic fibers and polyester fibers were developed about the same time, and the commercial development of both was postponed by World War Ⅱ Du Pont's synthesis of acrylic fiber evolved from the fundamental research of Dr. Carothers. Two distinct generic groups of fibers based on acrylonitrile chemistry are defined by the TFPIA:

(1) Acrylic fiber

Acrylic—a manufactured fiber in which the fiber-forming substance is any long-chain synthetic polymer composed of at least 85 percent by weight of acrylonitrile units.

The cross-section of acrylic and modacrylic fibers is determined by the method used for spinning the fiber. They can be round, or dogbone shape, or other shapes.

Acrylic fibers have medium tenacity and relatively high elongation and good recovery from small extensions. They have low moisture regain varying from 1.0% to 3.0%. Acrylic fibers melt on heating and generally exhibit a moderate flame propagation rate. They have good to moderate resistance to alkalies and acids and excellent resistance to sunlight.

Acrylic fibers are used extensively in carpets, furnishing fabrics, apparel (woven and knit fabrics).

(2) Modacrylic fiber

Modacrylic fiber is defined by the TFPIA as follows:

A manufactured fiber in which the fiber-forming substance is any long-chain synthetic polymer composed of less than 85 percent but at least 35 percent by weight of acrylonitrile units.

From its definition, it is apparent that modacrylics are modified acrylic fibers. Whereas in acrylic fibers up to 15 percent of a comonomer or other materials may be added to acrylonitrile, in modacrylics the comonomer may be the major constituent.

Modacrylic fibers are weaker than acrylics, although stronger than acetates. Abrasion resistance is very low. They have good resistance to organic solvents, although they do dissolve in acetone. Weak alkalies and acids do not affect the fiber. Sunlight resistance is poor.

Because of their excellent flame resistance characteristics, they are used in drapery and upholstery material. They also find use in carpets because of their good resiliency and rot and stain resistance.

5.4 Polyvinyl Chloride Fibers / 聚氯乙烯纤维

PVC fibers are smooth and have circular cross sections. They have good tensile properties, and not affected by acids or alkali and generally have excellent resistance to a wide range of chemicals. These fibers are used in a variety of textile applications. However, they find their properties exploited most usefully in industrial uses such as filter fabrics, wadding, tarpaulins, glider boats, etc. PVC fibers are also used in blends with wool, cotton, rayon, and nylon for apparel applications.

5.5 Polyvinyl Alcohol Fibers / 聚乙烯醇纤维

They have excellent tensile properties. These fibers have a smooth surface, and generally have a U shape cross-section with a flattened tube appearance. The latter characteristic makes them highly flexible, which results in a better feel and handle of fabrics. These fibers are used in all sorts of apparel applications such as suit interlinings, gloves, socks, and intimate garments.

5.6 Polyolefin Fibers / 聚烯烃纤维

The TFPIA defines olefin as follows:
A manufactured fiber in which the fiber-forming substance is any long-chain synthetic polymer composed of at least 85 percent by weight of ethylene, propylene, or other olefin units.

(1) Polyethylene Fibers

Because of higher crystallinity, high-density polyethylene fibers have a much higher tensile strength, stiffness, and higher softening point compared to the low-density polypropylene fibers. Nevertheless, they still can not be used effectively for general textile applications because of their low melting point, poor resilience and dyeing characteristics. However, because of their strength, rot resistance, and inertness to chemicals and light polyethylene fibers are used extensively in marine applications.

(2) Polypropylene

Polypropylene is the most usual member of olefin family in textile consumer goods. Polypropylene is produced not only by melt spinning but by the economical split-film method of fibrillating. The polymer is extruded in a sheet, which is then drawn and cut into narrow strips.

Polypropylene has the lowest density of any fiber, and so is very lofty, giving good cover for low price. Polypropylene fibers have excellent processing behavior because of their high fiber-to-fiber coefficient of friction and good crimp retention properties. They have excellent abrasion resistance and flex resistance. Above all, polypropylene fiber is the cheapest of all the synthetic fibers. In spite of almost no moisture absorbency, it wicks, so it has good static resistance. Low absorbency gives the fiber stain resistance in furnishing fabrics and quick drying in garments.

The fibers are extensively used in blankets, upholstery, and carpets. They are also used in the manufacture of fishnets, trawls, and lines. They are used in apparel application either in 100% pure form or in blends with rayon.

5.7　Spandex Fiber / 氨纶

Spandex is defined by the TFPIA as follows:

A manufactured fiber in which the fiber-forming substance is a long-chain synthetic polymer comprised of at least 85 percent by weight a segmented polyurethane.

Du Pont introduced a new stretch fiber in 1958. The name Lycra was given to the fiber in late 1959, and plans were announced for volume production. In the same year, U. S. Rubber introduced its new elastomer, Vyrene; production of that fiber ceased in the mid-1970s. Today the only producers of spandex fibers in the United States are the DuPont and Globe Manufacturing. The name Lycra is still used for DuPont's fiber; Glospan is the name of the Globe fiber.

Spandex fibers are generally stronger than ordinary rubber filaments. The tenacity of these fibers varies in the range of 4.4~13.2cN/tex as compared to 2.2 cN/tex for natural rubber. But they are also fairly weak. Their breaking elongation may vary up to 700%, and they demonstrate excellent recovery behavior. They have very low moisture regain, which may vary from 1.0% to 1.3%. Spandex fibers have a good resistance to acids, alkalies, and most common chemicals.

Spandex fibers are used in swimwear, foundation garments, support hosiery, sock tops, elastic webbing for waistbands, and other similar uses. There is a great deal of interest in the use of spandex in active-sportswear fabric.

5.8 Aramid / 芳纶

Aramid is another type of polyamide fibers. In this type of fibers, at least 85% of the amide linkages are attached directly to two aromatic rings.

The two major types of aramid fibers are Nomex and Kevlar. The production of aramid fibers uses a solvent spinning process.

The strength and heat resistance of the aramid fibers are the properties of major interest to consumers of these fibers. Kevlar is the strongest of the fibers, with a tenacity of 198 cN/tex. It is approximately five times stronger than a steel wire of the same weight, and more than twice as strong as high-tenacity industrial nylon, polyester, or fiber glass. At temperatures above 370℃ Nomex degrades; the behavior of Kevlar is similar.

The above combination of properties makes these fibers particularly suited for end-use applications such as hot air filtration, protective clothing, military applications (helmets and bullet-proof vests), and structural supports for aircrafts and boats. Other uses include ropes and cables, mechanical rubber goods, and marine and sporting goods equipment.

Other types

There are various other types of man-made fibers such as glass, ceramic, metallic, and carbon, including such generic types as novoloid (kynol), anidex, nytrill, azelon, etc., that are currently being manufactured.

Glossary of Technical Terms / 专业词汇：

polyamide	聚酰胺
polyester	聚酯
Imperial Chemical Industries(ICI)	帝国工业公司
condensation reaction	缩聚反应
polymerization	聚合反应
multifilament	复丝
monofilament	单丝
ester group	酯基

pill	起球
orifice	喷丝孔
spinnerette (spinneret)	喷丝板
heat-setting	热定形
aromatic ring	芳香环
aramid	芳纶
initial modulus	初始模量
elastomeric fiber	弹性纤维
polyurethane	聚氨基甲酸酯
polyacrylic	聚丙烯腈
modacrylic fiber	改性丙烯腈纤维
polyvinyl chloride fiber	聚氯乙烯纤维
polyvinyl alcohol fiber	聚乙烯醇纤维
spandex	氨纶

Questions / 思考题：

1. Describe the main characteristics of Nylon.
2. What will happen when the Dacron polyester is ignited?
3. Describe the main properties of acrylic fibers.

Activities / 实践作业：

1. What three synthetic fibers are present in most of your own clothing? Make up a table showing the article, the fiber content, the types of fibers that it blended with, and the properties of that fiber that make it suitable for that use.

2. List the major advantages and disadvantages of polyester/cotton blend fabrics for apparel use.

3. Relatively small amounts of spandex yarns included with yarns made from other fibers allow woven cloths to stretch. Give three examples of your clothing in which stretch woven cloth would be useful, and give the amount of spandex.

Chapter Six
Yarn / 纱线

Objectives / 学习目标：

1. Define a yarn.
2. State and classify the different types of yarn and their uses.
3. Recognize different types of yarns.
4. Describe the characteristic yarn of yarns.

Maybe you can knit a sweater or scarf, at least you have seen other people do this. For this you use a long thread, untwist the thread and observe it. You will find that it is made of a bundle of fibers. This thread made of fibers can be called a yarn. Can you now define a yarn?

The word yarn is derived from the Anglo-Saxon word *gearn* and bears resemblance to Old High German's *garn* yarn, Greek's *chordē* string, and Sanskrit's *hira* band. The ASTM D123 defines textile yarns as "a generic term for a continuous strand of textile fibers, filaments, or others material in a form suitable for weaving, knitting or otherwise intertwining to form a textile fabric". Yarns can make from both natural (such as wool, linen, cotton) and synthetic fibers (such as rayon, polyester, nylon), in filament or staple form, suitable for use in the production of textiles, such as knitting, weaving, sewing, crocheting, embroidery, and ropemaking so on.

6.1 Classification of Yarns / 纱线分类

The subject of yarns comes to a very wide field and various methods of classification so that the subject should be intelligently considered, the yarn maybe simple or fancy, single strands or multiple-plies, smooth or fuzzy, glossy or dull. The variety of yarns is almost endless.

6.1.1 Classification According to the Length of Fibers / 按照纤维长度分类

6.1.1.1 Staple Yarns / 短纤纱

Staple or spun yarns are made from staple fibers. Being short they are held together by twisting in order to form a long continuous strand (Fig. 6-1). In general there are two main system of preparing fiber for yarn. When it comes to wool, system are known as worsted and woollen system. For cotton, it is called carded or combed system.

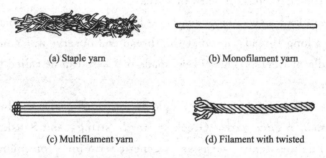

(a) Staple yarn   (b) Monofilament yarn

(c) Multifilament yarn   (d) Filament with twisted

Fig. 6-1 Types of yarn according to fibers length

Almost all man-made fibers are produced as continuous filaments. When these have to be blended with cotton or wool, they are cut into the desired short length and blended yarns are produced from the blended fibers. The most popular blend of this type is that of polyester staple fiber with cotton, blended usually in proportions of 65/35 or 50/50.

6.1.1.2 Filament Yarn / 长丝纱

It is made from long continuous filaments. Monofilament yarns are made from a single, relatively thicker filament fiber. Transparent sewing thread, metallic yarns, bare elastic, and fishing lines are examples of monofilament yarns. Multifilament yarns are made by aggregating many filaments together. They can be given low twist or high twist (Fig. 6-1).

6.1.2 Classification According to the Structure of Yarns / 按照纱线结构分类

6.1.2.1 Simple Yarns / 普通纱线

Simple yarns have uniform size and regular surface. They are even in size and have an equal number of turns per unit length throughout their length and are relatively smooth. Simple yarns are further classified into three types (Fig. 6-2).

(1) Single yarn

It is made from simple assemblage of filament or staple fibers evenly twisted together. It is suitable for operations such as weaving and knitting.

(2) Ply yarn

When two or more simple single yarns are twisted together, they are called ply yarns. They are termed two-ply, three ply, four ply and so on, according to the number of simple single yarns twisted together.

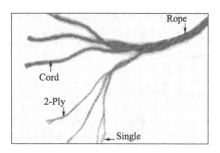

Fig. 6-2 The structure of simple yarn

(3) Cord yarn and rope yarn

When two or more ply yarns are twisted together, the resultant yarn is called cord. And, rope yarn is produced by twisting two or more cord yarns.

6.1.2.2 Complex/Novelty yarns / 花式纱线

Typically complex yarns are the uneven yarns which may be thick and thin or have curls, loops, twists and even differently coloured areas along their length. Due to this fancy look of the yarns they are used to add interesting decorative surface effects in fabrics. We can also call them novelty yarn or fancy yarn. The demand for yarns with structural and/or optical effects is due to the special aesthetic and high decorative appeal to the woven, knitted materials, and other textiles as well.

Fancy yarns find numerous applications in women's dress materials, men's suiting and casting, upholstery and furnishing fabrics, curtains and rags etc. Fancy yarns may have a number of features such as surface characteristics, count, colour or combination of colours, material, direction of twist etc. Usually, Fancy yarns are produced with a multiplicity of structural features but the structure of a fancy yarn may be considered in terms of the following three basic components: the base or core yarn, the fancy effect yarn, the binder yarn (Fig. 6-3).

The fancy effect yarn is wrapped around the core yarn to form the design. The binder yarn holds the effect yarn in place on the base to prevent it from slipping while it is being wound, woven or knitted. Generally fancy yarns contain at least two of these features. Derivatives of novelty yarn are as follows:

(1) Slub yarn

Slub Yarn (Fig. 6-4) is a yarn containing thick places of different thickness and length that is achieved by programmed acceleration of back and middle rollers in case of ring spinning and the feed roller in case of rotor spinning, at the same time maintaining the front roller at a constant speed. This controlled acceleration produces variation in the count of the base yarn. The random variation of thickness, length and pause gives a wide range of effects, ensuring the use of slub yarns in many applications like denim, shirting, knitwear, casual wear, ladies dress material and also in curtains and upholstery.

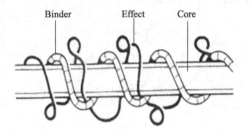

Fig. 6-3 The structure of Fancy yarns

Fig. 6-4 Slub yarn

(2) Covered yarn

Covered yarn has a core yarn that is completely covered by fiber or another yarn. Fig 6-5 shows different types of covered yarns. The core might be an elastomeric yarn,

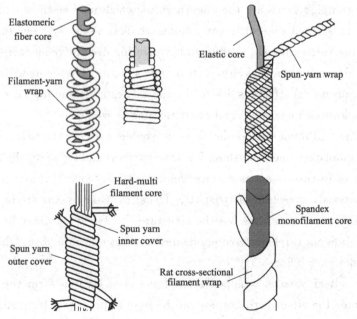

Fig. 6-5 Structure of different types covered yarn

such as rubber or spandex, or yarns, such as polyester or nylon. Covered yarns may have either a single covering or double covering. The second covering is usually twisted in the direction opposite from the first covering.

(3) Eyelash yarn

Eyelash yarn (Fig. 6-6) is made from a polyester fiber with a furry texture resembling eyelashes. These novelty yarns are made of a thin central ply surrounded by short "hairs". This yarn differs from "fur" type yarn in that it contains evenly spaced threads at intervals between lengths of bare core thread, whereas fur yarns have an abundance of threads covering the entirety of the core thread. Eyelash yarn comes in a wide range of colors, with the "hairs" sometimes being made of multicolored or metallic fibers.

Fig. 6-6　Eyelash yarn

(4) Bouclé yarn

It is a yarn with a length of loops of similar size which can range from tiny circlets to large curls. To make bouclé, at least two strands are combined, with the tension on one strand being much looser than the other as it is being plied, with the loose strand forming the wavy projections on its surface. Both gimp yarns and loop yarns belong to the bouclé groups (Fig. 6-7).

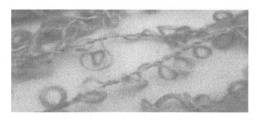 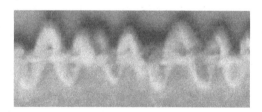

(a) Loop yarn　　　　　　　　　　　　　　(b) Gimp yarn

Fig. 6-7　Bouclé yarn

(5) Snarl yarn

Snarl yarn is similar to loop yarn except that the looping yarn has high twist so that the loop turns into a snarl (Fig. 6-8).

(6) Ladder yarn

Ladder resembles a ladder (Fig. 6-9), with two flat threads representing the two sides of the ladder held together by a strip of material at the center that represents the rungs. The material at the center of ladder yarn can be metallic, beaded, or otherwise adorned. This type of yarn is more often used to create trim or embellishments than to knit or crochet entire garments.

 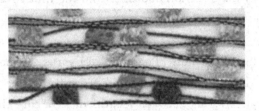

Fig. 6-8 Snarl yarn   Fig. 6-9 Ladder yarn

(7) Knot yarn

A nub yarn or knot yarn (Fig. 6-10) is created by tightly twisting an effect fiber around the base fiber. The nub is most easily identified when the effect and base yarns are of different colors.

(8) Spiral yarn

The appearance of corkscrew or spiral yarns is achieved by using yarns of two different fibers and often twisting one under a different tension than the other (Fig. 6-11).

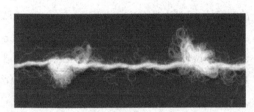 

Fig. 6-10 Knot yarn   Fig. 6-11 Spiral yarn

(9) Chenille yarn

The soft, fuzzy surface of chenille yarns (Fig. 6-12), which resemble pipe cleaners in appearance, can be created in several ways. Most commonly, a fabric is first produced and then cut into narrow strips resembling a yarn. Then, when the fabric is cut, the raw edges become very fuzzy and produce the chenille appearance. Other chenilles are created by trimming a loosely attached effect fiber to create the fuzzy appearance. Still other chenilles are created by attaching or gluing fibers to the yarn.

Fig. 6-12 Chenille yarn

(10) Metallic yarn

Metallic yarn is often classified as fancy yarn and is created by adding a metallic fiber or yarn to the blend. These are not to be confused with actual wire used in jewelry that is sometimes knit or crocheted.

(11) Crepe yarn

Crepe yarn may be classified as fancy yarn and is created by tightening the twist given to a yarn, resulting in a kinked or looped strand.

(12) Diamond yarn

A diamond yarn (Fig. 6-13) is produced by folding a coarse single yarn or roving with a fine yarn or filament having contrasting color using S-twist, and cabling it with a similar fine yarn using Z-twist.

(13) Ribbon or tape yarn

The yarn is not produced by spinning. It is finely knitted tubes, pressed flat to resemble ribbon or tape. The ribbons are usually soft, shiny and silky (Fig. 6-14).

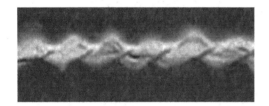

Fig. 6-13　Diamond yarn   Fig. 6-14　Ribbon yarn

6.1.2.3　Textured Yarns / 变形纱

Texturing is the formation of folds, loops, coils, or crinkles in filaments. Flat continuous filament yarns made from thermoplastic materials can be made permanently bulky by various processes. Nylon and polyester are two main fibers that are textured. Such alterations in the physical shape of a fiber have an effect on the behavior and hand of textiles made from them. Hand, or handle, is an all-purpose term for the characteristics perceived by the sense of touch when a fabric is held in the fingers, such as drapability, smoothness, flexibility.

(1) The characteristic of textured yarn

① increased volume;

② better thermal insulation due to the enclosed air;

③ increased extensibility and elasticity;

④ higher vapour permeability and moisture transport;

⑤ lower luster;

⑥ softer and more comfortable fabrics.

(2) The texturing processes and their products

① False-twist texturing   The false twist texturing method is a U. S. -patented textile process. The method uses machines that twist, heat-treat and untwist synthetic yarn to create a bulkier and softer finished product (Fig. 6-15).

② Air-jet texturing   Invented by DuPont, in this method of texturing, yarn is led through the turbulent region of an air jet at a rate faster than it is drawn off on the far side of the jet. In the jet, the yarn structure is opened, loops are formed, and the structure is closed again. Some loops are locked inside and others are locked on the surface of the yarn. The processing increases the bulk of the yarn and the twist is locked in after the air-jet texturing. Since this is a process of mechanical interlocking, this sort of texturing can be used on all sorts of yarn. Blending of yarns is also possible with this method. An example of this method is the Taslan process (Fig. 6-16).

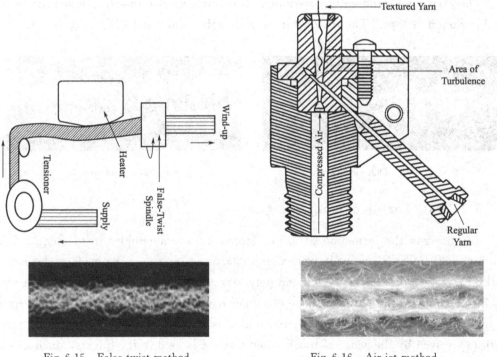

Fig. 6-15   False-twist method   Fig. 6-16   Air-jet method

③ Stuffer-box texturing   The crimping unit consists of two feed rolls and a brass tube stuffer box. By compressing the yarn into the heated stuffer box, the individual fi laments are caused to fold or bend at a sharp angle, while being simultaneously set by a heating device (Fig. 6-17).

④ Edge crimping /Knife edge texturing   In this method of texturing, thermoplastic yarns in a heated and stretched condition are drawn over a crimping edge and cooled (Fig. 6-18). Edge-crimping machines are used to make Agilon yarns.

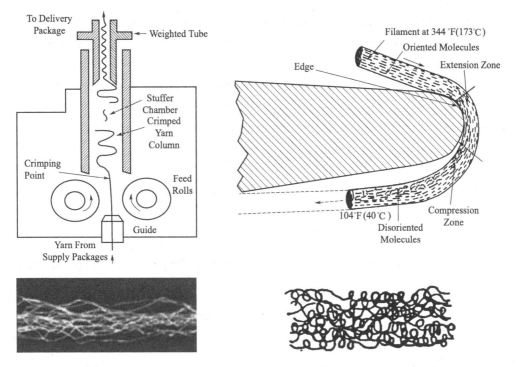

Fig. 6-17　Stuffer-box method　　　　Fig. 6-18　Edge crimping method

⑤ Gear crimping texturing　In this texturing method, yarn is fed through the meshing teeth of two gears. The yarn takes on the shape of the gear teeth (Fig. 6-19).

⑥ Knit-de-knit texturing　In this method of texturing, the yarn is knit into a 2-inch diameter hose-leg, heat-set in an autoclave, and then unraveled and wound onto a final package. This texturing method produces a crinkle yarn (Fig. 6-20).

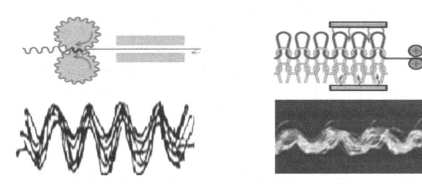

Fig. 6-19　Gear crimping method　　　　Fig. 6-20　Knit-de-knit method

(3) Types of textured yarn

Whatever the texturing process used, textured yarns can be classified into three groups:

① Stretch yarns Highly elastic yarns with a crimp extension of 150% to 300%.

② Stabilised yarns Yarns which have been given an additional setting treatment to reduce their elasticity and crimp extension.

③ Bulked yarns Voluminous yarns with crimps and loops having normal extensibility and elasticity. The term bulked yarn is often used generally to cover all continuous filament textured yarns and bulked staple fiber yarns.

6.1.3 Classification of Yarns According to Counts / 按照纱线细度分类

Yarns are frequently spoken of as fine, medium, or coarse. It may be stated that, in general, cotton yarns are considered coarse up to 30s, from 30s to 60s they are referred to as medium numbers, and from 60s upwards as fine yarns.

6.1.4 Classification of Yarns According to their Preparation / 按照加工过程分类

In preparation for spinning, yarn may be carded, combed, or condensed. Yarn is also distinguished according to the type of machine on which it is spun (ring spinning, open-end spinning). A distinction is also made between raw yarn (without any finish), bleached yarn, mercerized yarn, dyed yarn, and mélange yarn (a mixture of dyed and raw fibers).

There are three basic types of cotton yarns. Combed cotton yarns, the finest cotton yarns, have a thickness of 5~18.5 tex and are made primarily of fine-stapled cotton. Carded cotton yarn has a thickness of 13.3~100 tex and is made of middle-grade cotton. Condensed cotton yarn, which has a thickness of 100 tex or greater, is made from cotton wastes and low-grade cotton.

Wool yarn is manufactured in thicknesses of 15.5~42 tex (combed), 30~83 tex (coarse combed), and 42~500 tex (condensed).

Linen yarn is spun by the dry method from long and short flax fiber and tow or by the wet method (the roving is moistened before spinning) from long fiber and tow. Yarn having a thickness of 24~200 tex is produced by wet spinning, and coarse yarn with a thickness of 33~666 tex is usually produced by dry spinning. Coarse linen yarn is also produced when other types of bast fibers are spun (hemp, jute).

6.2 Structure and Characteristics / 纱线结构与性能

6.2.1 Yarn Size / 纱线细度

The yarn size or yarn count expresses the thickness of the yarn, and must be known before calculating the quantity of yarns for a known length of fabric. The yarn count number indicates the length of yarn in relation to the weight. There are three systems of yarn count are currently in use:

① The fixed weight system (Nm): is used for numbering spun yarns. It is based on the length of the yarn per 1.0 gram and is measured in metric (Nm). With Nm, the number to the right of the diagonal stroke reveals the number of individual yarns (folding number) that are contained in the ply-yarn.

Example: Nm 80/2 (2 yarns, each of 80 m, weigh 2 g).

② The English Cotton Count systems (Ne): the yarn number for cotton yarns is based on the number of 840-yard hanks in a pound. The convention for indicating plies resembles that for wool. Two-ply 20s would be written 2/20s or 20/2, and would be twice the weight, length for length, of single ply 20s yarn.

③ The fixed length system: In fixed length system, such as the denier and tex systems, the numerical solution to the equation increases as the yarn gets thicker. Thus, there is a direct relationship between yarn number and yarn size. The length of material remains constant and the mass changes. The constant length used in the denier system is 9000meters; in the tex system it is 1000 meters, if 9000 meters of a yarn weighs 9grams, it is a 9-denier or 1-tex yarn; if 1000 meters of it weighs 9 grams, it is a 9-tex or an 81-denier yarn.

Both ASTM and the International Standards Organization (ISO) have recommended the tex system as the standard yarn numbering system. A major reason for its adoption is the ease with which yarn numbers can be calculated by simply measuring a length of yarn and then carefully weighting it.

The adoption of a universal yarn numbering system would simplify the description of such properties as strength and cost. It would become unnecessary to convert yarn breaking strength in pounds to grams per denier in order to compare data collected by two different systems. Manufacturers could simplify the costing of production operations if the same system of fiber and yarn numbering were used for all operations.

6.2.2 Yarn Evenness / 纱线细度均匀度

Yarn evenness deals with the variation in yarn fineness. This is the property, commonly measured as the variation in mass per unit length along the yarn, is a basic and important one, since it can influence so many other properties of the yarn and of fabric made from it. Such variations are inevitable, because they arise from the fundamental nature of textile fibers and from their resulting arrangement.

Irregularity can adversely affect many of the properties of textile materials. The most obvious consequence of yarn evenness is the variation of strength along the yarn. The uneven one should have more thin regions than the even one as a result of irregula rity, since the average linear density is the same. A second quality-related effect of uneven yarn is the presence of visible faults on the surface of fabrics. If a large amount of irregularity is present in the yarn, the variation in fineness can easily be detected in the finished cloth. The problem is particularly serious when a fault (i. e a thick or thin place) appears at precisely regular intervals along the length of the yarn.

The mass per unit length variation due to variation in fiber assembly is generally known as "IRREGULARITY" or "UNEVENNESS". It is true that the diagram can represent a true reflection of the mass or weight per unit length variation in a fiber assembly. For a complete analysis of the quality, however, the diagram alone is not enough. It is also necessary to have a numerical value which represents the mass variation. The mathematical statistics offer 2 methods:

(1) The irregularity U%

It is the percentage mass deviation of unit length of material and is caused by uneven fiber distribution along the length of the strand.

(2) The coefficient of variation C. V. %

In handling large quantities of data statistically, the coefficient of variation (C. V. %) is commonly used to define variability and is thus well-suited to the problem of expressing yarn evenness. It is currently probably the most widely accepted way of quantifying irregularity.

It is given by coefficient variation(C. V. %)=(standard deviation/average)×100

6.2.3　Imperfections / 纱疵

Imperfections is the description for thin, thick places and neps in 1000m of yarn.

(1) Thin places

Thin places are places in the yarn, that are thinner than −50% or more than the average diameter of the yarn. There is no limitation in the length of the thin place. The less you find thin places in the yarn the better is it.

(2) Thick places

Thick places are determined where the yarn diameter is in excess of 50% of the average yarn diameter and the length is 8～12 mm.

(3) Neps

It has to be made a differentiation in the two faults—thick places and neps. Frequently-occurring thick places exhibit a length that corresponds with the mean staple length of the fiber. A nep is a very short thick place in the yarn, a small fault having a length of 2mm diameter of 3 times or more at a standard setting of 200%. It can either be a fiber nep, a seed coat nep or a trash particle. It can be thicker than +200% of the average yarn diameter. The increase for neps is calculated to a reference length of 1mm. They can be a bunch of entangled fibers commonly not bigger than pin ball head.

6.2.4 Yarn Hairiness / 纱线毛羽

Yarn hairiness denotes the amount of hairs (fibers) protruding above the surface of the textile yarn. Especially, in case of staple spun yarns, since multiple fibers are bound in a single yarn, fibers will tend to protrude outside the body of the yarn even though proper twisting is done for that yarn.

Usually hairiness is denoted in terms of the parameter 'H', which means 'Hairiness Index'. It represents the total length of hairs (in cm) measured over the yarn length of 1 cm.

Another way of representing Hairiness is "Hair Count". It represents the number of hairs counted for a given length of yarn. It varies from 3mm to 10mm. Longer hairs are problematic compared to shorter hairs. Shorter hairs are essential for yarns to provide comfort for fabrics.

In new generation testers, a new parameter called "Hair Severity" is available which represents the severity of longer hairs. This number will indicate the influence of hairs in further processing like weaving and knitting.

6.2.5 Yarn Twist / 纱线加捻

Yarns are twisted to hold the fibers together. The number of twists per unit length is used to measure twist. Yarn twist can be broadly divided by number of twists: none or very low, low, average, and high twist. Yarn twist impacts the yarn's appearance, fineness, strength, and absorption. Fibres can be twisted together in the clockwise or counter clockwise direction to form yarns. Yarns are twisted in the clockwise direction for "S" twist, and counter clockwise for "Z" twist. The "Z" twist is employed in a majority of the spun yarns used for fabric construction. Depending on the direction of this final twist, the yarn will be known as S-twist or Z-twist (Fig. 6-21).

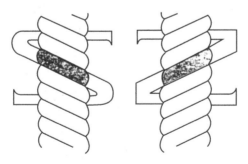

Fig. 6-21 Directions of twist

The strength of a thread twisted from staple fibers increases with increasing twist. In the lower portion of the curve (Fig. 6-22), this strength will be solely due to sliding friction, i.e. under tensile loading the fibers tend to slide apart.

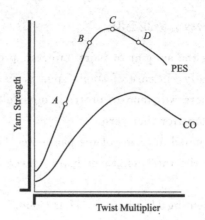

Fig. 6-22　Effect of Yarn Twist on Yarn Strength

Cohesive friction arises only in the middle-to-upper regions of the curve. This is caused by the high tension, and thus high pressure, and finally becomes so considerable that fewer and fewer fibers slide past each other and more and more are broken. This continues up to a certain maximum, is dependent upon the raw material.

Glossary of Technical Terms / 专业词汇：

sewing thread	缝纫线
twine	麻线，绳子
cord	绳，索
thread	线
ply yarn	合股线
ply	纱线股数
monofilament	单纤，单纤丝
multifilament	复丝，多纤维丝
novelty yarn/fancy yarn	花式纱线
hawser	粗绳，缆
cable	巨缆
numbering system	细度计量制
yarn number/yarn count	纱线支数
fixed length system	定长制
fixed weight system	定重制
skein	绞纱
worsted count/woolen run	粗纺毛纱支数
twist	捻度，捻回
twist per inch	每英寸捻数
spinning frame	细纱机

twist multiplier	捻系数
evenness	均匀度
nep	棉结，白星，毛粒
slub	粗节，糙粒
core-spun yarn	包芯纱
lively yarn	绉缩纱
seed yarn	疙瘩花线
spiral yarn	螺旋花线
boucle yarn	结子纱线
nub yarn	结子纱线，疙瘩花饰线
loop yarn	起圈花线
diamond-metallic core	菱形—金属芯
slub yarn	竹节花式纱线
chenile	雪尼尔线
visual and tactile characteristics	目测手感特性
split film yarn	裂膜纱线
glass yarn	玻璃丝
wire yarn	金属丝
jet stream texturizing	喷气变形工艺
differential bulk effect	变异蓬松化效应
stuffer box	填塞箱法
false-twist stretch filament yarn	假捻弹力丝
bulkiness	蓬松度
nonlinearity	非线性
elastomeric yarns	弹性纱
false twist	假捻

Questions / 思考题：

1. What is the difference between a staple fiber and a staple fiber yarn?
2. How can yarn be spun by hand?
3. What is the importance of twist for a yarn?
4. How many types of yarn twist are you aware of?
5. Which would you expect to be the stronger yarn, a 60/3 or a 40/1? Explain your answer.
6. How does twist affect the fabric properties?
7. Write an essay on textured yarns and their characteristics.
8. What is the structure of a fancy textured yarn?
9. What effect do fancy yarns have on performance of fabrics containing these

yarns?

10. Define a fancy yarn.

11. What are the three components of a fancy yarn and what are their functions?

12. Name the three groups into which all fancy yarns can be classified.

Activities / 实践作业：

1. Take 10 fabrics with different appearances and softness. Remove individual warp and weft yarns from the fabric and observe the yarns by putting them independently on a flat surface. What do you notice? Untwist these warp and weft yarns. What is your observation?

2. Collect some yarn samples to show varying levels of twist and size.

3. Visit the local department stores and shops. Survey the type of yarns (simple spun, textured and untextured filament, complex) used in the following end uses：

Men's and women's daytime wear, men's and women's evening wear, children's playclothes, children's sleeping clothes.

4. Collect samples of fabrics made from simple filaments, simple yarns, and novelty yarns.

Chapter Seven
Yarn Manufacturing / 纺纱加工

Objectives / 学习目标：

1. Understand how yarns are manufactured from staple fibers.
2. Understand the role of twist in determining the properties of a yarn.
3. Understanding the modification of Ring Spun systems.
4. Understand the principle of non-conventional spun systems.

7.1 History of Yarn / 纱线的发展史

Spinning fiber into yarn is such an ancient art that its origins are lost in the mists of time. That's not an exaggeration; the oldest recovered artifacts made with 'yarn' are string skirts that date up to 20,000 years ago. Yarn was initially a by-product of wool and its thought early man invented the art of twisting the strands out and making fibers. Cotton fibers have been used by mankind for over 5000 years. Much before mechanized spinning became possible; yarns were made from cotton by hand. The high spinnability of cotton can be demonstrated by taking a small bunch of fibers and then rolling them in one direction in the palms of your hands when it gets converted into a coarse cotton yarn. By 5,000 BC spindles began to appear. This is estimated to be about 1,000 years before the invention of the wheel, which gives you some idea of how ancient they are.

It was the invention of the spinning wheel that revolutionized the manufacture of yarn and textiles, and in fact, the world. No one knows for certain where or when the first spinning wheels were made. Some believe they originated in India between 500 and 1000 AD. These early spinning wheels—which are still in use today—are called Charkha wheels, has been developed and is quite extensively used to make hand-spun cotton yarn for making fabric.

7.2 Traditional Spinning / 传统纺纱

There are three major spinning processes: cotton, worsted or long-staple, or wool. Synthetic staple fibers can be made with any of these processes. Since more yarn is produced with the cotton process than the other two, its manufacture is described below.

7.2.1 Opening and Cleaning / 开清棉

Fibers are shipped in bales, which are opened by hand or machine. Natural fibers may require cleaning, whereas synthetic fibers only require separating. The picker loosens and separates the lumps of fiber and also cleans the fiber if necessary. Blending of different staple fibers may be required for certain applications. Blending may be done during formation of the lap, during carding, or during drawing out. Quantities of each fiber are measured carefully and their proportions are consistently maintained.

The main task of opening room is to open the big flocks to small tufts, cleaning

i. e. trash removing, fiber mixing and even feed for carding machine. The Fig. 7-1 shows the Rieter opening line, and the Fig. 7-2 show the Trutschler modular opening component line.

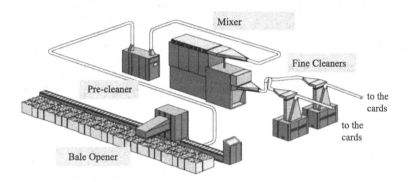

Fig. 7-1　Rieter opening line

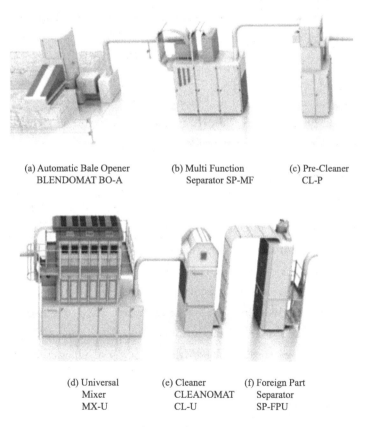

Fig. 7-2　Trutschler modular opening component line

The Different machines comprising the opining line are multi-functional. The typical Trützschler compact installations lies in four components: bale opening, installation protection, mixing and cleaning, foreign part separation and dust.

7.2.2 Carding / 梳棉

There is no processing stage that changes the form, assignment, condition, and composition of the cotton so strongly as the carding process does. Opened and cleaned materials arrive at the carding stage in the form of small tufts composed of entangled fibers. The purpose of the carding stage is to disentangle these tufts into a collection of individual fibers, the collection being in the form of a web of fibers, and then to consolidate this collection into a sliver. Rate of production and quality should be optimized.

7.2.3 Combing / 精梳

When a smoother, finer yarn is required, fibers are subjected to a further paralleling method. A comblike device arranges fibers into parallel form, with short fibers falling out of the strand.

Tasks of combing:

(1) Elimination of precisely pre-determined quantity of short fibers.
(2) Elimination of the remaining impurities.
(3) Elimination of a large proportion of the neps.
(4) Formation of a sliver having maximum possible evenness.
(5) Producing of more straight and parallel fibers.
(6) Elimination of short fibers improves mainly the staple length Micronaire value of combed sliver is slightly higher than that of feedstock.

7.2.4 Drawing / 并条

After carding or combing, the fiber mass is referred to as the sliver. Several slivers are combined before this process. A series of rollers rotating at different rates of speed elongate the sliver into a single more uniform strand that is given a small amount of twist and fed into large cans. Carded slivers are drawn twice after carding. Combed slivers are drawn once before combing and twice more after combing.

Fig. 7-3 shows Trützschler autoleveller draw frame TD8, Its self-optimizing function OPTI SET is a standard feature that automatically determines the optimum value by considering such parameters as machine settings, material characteristics and ambient atmosphere.

7.2.5 Roving / 粗纱

After the single or several stages of drawing (as the case may be for combed sliver), the sliver is taken to a "slubber" where it is drawn out further to the desired shape, twisted and then wound on bobbins. These bobbins are then placed on the intermediate frame, where further drawing and twisting takes place.

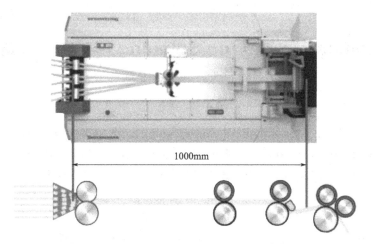

Fig. 7-3 Trützschler autoleveller draw frame TD8

The sliver is fed through a machine called the roving frame, where the strands of fiber are further elongated and given additional twist. These strands are called the roving.

Tasks of roving frame:

(1) Attenuation the sliver to a fine strand.

(2) A protective twist must be inserted, that the roving can be wound on a package transported.

(3) Roving winding makes the roving frame relatively complex winding requires in addition to the spindle and flyer, a cone drive transmission (or variable gear), a differential gear and a builder motion.

7.2.6 Ring Spinning / 细纱

Next the yarn is placed on the ring spinning frame, where it passes through several sets of rollers running at successively higher speeds and is finally drawn out or drafted by introducing twist and winding operations. The yarn here passes through a traveller to a spindle which revolves and puts in an exact number of twists as the yarn is wound up on a desired bobbin. The ring spinning frame completes the manufacture of yarn by drawing out, inserting twist, winding the yarn, all in one operation.

The production of staple or spun yarn is not limited to yarns from one kind of fiber alone. Blends of cotton with polyester and of wool with polyester are well known. Polyester is also blended with other fibers in varying proportions. The main reasons for the increasing use of polyester blend with cotton fibers are the easy care and wash and wear characteristics imparted by the polyester component. In addition, it also imparts durability, strength, wrinkle resistance and elastic recovery to the composite yarn. For carpets, blend of wool with acrylic fibers is quite popular.

7.3 Modification of Ring Spinning / 环锭纺纱改造

7.3.1 Compact Spinning / 紧密纺

Compact spinning is essentially a ring spinning with additional feature to eliminate or reduce yarn hairiness in the so called condensing zone. This is done to improve surface integrity and increase yarn strength. The spinning triangle is reduced or eliminated to condensing the fibers in a narrow path. The close and parallel device is closely situated before the twist imparting. Compact spinning offers near perfect structure by applying air suction or magnetic system for condensing the fibers before twisting, thereby eliminating of the spinning triangle, as shown in Fig. 7-4.

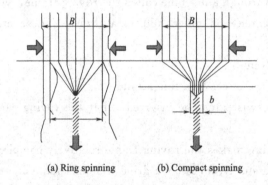

(a) Ring spinning   (b) Compact spinning

Fig. 7-4 Spinning triangles in ring and compact spinning

Compact spinning has been shown to significantly improve yarn tensile properties and reduction in yarn hairiness. Fig. 7-5 shown the hairness of the yarn.

 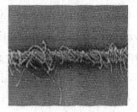

Fig. 7-5 Hairness over the conventional and compact yarns

Both characteristics are crucial for performance in downstream manufacturing operations. There are several famous compact spinning systems are as follow: Rieter Com4 Compact Spinning System, which is the first compact spinning system to be commercialized and only for use with extra-long-staple cottons to make only the very fine yarn sizes (i. e., 50 Ne and finer). Both Sussen Elite Compact Spinning System and

Zinser Compact System are designed to accommodate the full spectrum of staple lengths spun today.

7.3.2 SiroSPUN / 赛洛纺

The SiroSPUN™ process adapted some of the self-twist discoveries of CSIRO to the ring spinning technology of the worsted system, and combined spinning and doubling in the one operation. The technology maintains two separate strands during the spinning process, as shown in Fig. 7-6, and this allows a number of fiber-binding mechanisms to operate before the strands are twisted about each other. An important aspect of the SiroSPUN™ system is a simple device to break out the remaining strand if one of the strands should be accidentally broken.

Fig. 7-6　SiroSPUN spinning process

SiroSPUN™ is used also for short staple fibers as cotton and blends. The roving strands, which are drafted parallel, are combined after passing the front rollers at the exit from the drafting system, with some twist being produced in the individual strands right up to the nip point. Once past the front roller of the drafting system, the two strands are combined producing a twofold-like yarn. The yarn has uni-directional twist like a singles yarn but the fibers are bound sufficiently for the yarn to survive weaving.

7.3.3 Sirofil / 赛洛菲尔纺

Sirofil spinning has been developed from sirospun and CSIRO first studied the sirofil spinning. Sirofil spinning uses a filament yarn and a staple fiber roving, which are fed separately and kept a fixed distance to the nip of the front drafting roller (Fig. 7-7).

7.3.4 Solospun / 缆型纺

Solospun yarn is a singles worsted yarn which can be woven as a warp without plying, sizing or any other yarn finishing treatment. To achieve this, the fiber geometry

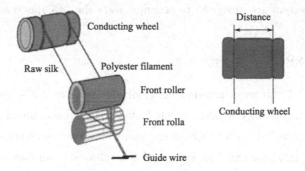

Fig. 7-7   Sirofil spinning process

within the yarn structure is modified so that all the fibers are securely bound within the yarn. The resulting Solospun yarn has a very high level of resistance to the abrasive forces imposed by the weaving process. Solospun yarns are made using a small patented roller attachment which simply clips onto the shaft of the front drafting roller (Fig. 7-8). It does not affect the normal operation of the machine and is compatible with auto-doffing mechanisms. Roller life is expected to be more than six months in a typical production operation.

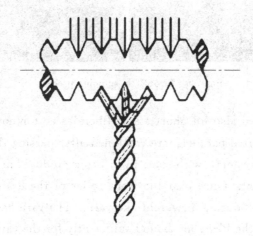

Fig. 7-8   Solospun system

Solospun units are easily fitted or removed from the spinning frame. Easily set up on most spinning frames. Fits all drafting arms. Fit 100 spindles in one hour. Independent adjustment of roller position and pressure. Tenacity, extensibility and evenness of Solospun yarns are not much different from conventional two-fold weaving yarns. Yarn cross-section is more circular than two-fold yarn so Solospun yarn is a little harder and less bulky. Solospun yarns are less hairy than conventional singles yarns because the individual fibers are bound securely into the body of the yarn at several points along the fiber length. Fiber ends are far less likely to be rubbed up as 'hairs'.

Woven cloth has a smoother finish and cleaner appearance.

7.4 New Methods of Spinning System / 新型纺纱

7.4.1 Introduction / 引言

In today's technology, many spinning systems are used commercially to produce spun yarns with a wide range of values of characteristics. Among these systems, ring spinning enjoys the greatest diversity and the highest quality levels. Ring spinning has been able to supplant almost all other conventional spinning methods and has proved very resistant to inroads by the newcomers. This can be attributed mainly to its flexibility, universal applicability, and yarn quality.

Other new spinning systems such as rotor spinning, air-jet spinning, and friction spinning suffer inherent limitations that make them suitable for only narrow ranges of yarn count and twist levels. However, the major limiting factor in ring spinning is their low production rate in comparison with all new spinning technologies. Typically, ring-spinning can only operate at a production speed of up to 30 m/min, while other systems producing comparable yarns (such as rotor spinning and air-jet spinning) can operate at production speeds of up to 250 m/min. The low production rate in ring spinning is primarily attributed to the use of the ring/traveller system for twisting and win ding.

Search for new solutions offers the prospect of basic advances in the spinning field in future. The research on non-conventional spinning system began on a broad front at the end of the 1960s. The newer spinning systems developed since then include rotor spinning, air-jet spinning, friction spinning, vortex spinning, electrostatic spinning, core spinning, wrap spinning, twistless spinning and others. The structures of yarn obtained from these systems are also different and vary in many aspects. The ring yarns have helical structure and even twist distribution, but sometimes there can be problem in ring spun yarn related to twist liveliness and migration of fibers inside yarn. For improving these aspect new structures came into picture, which are different from ring spun yarn structure and these structures will also behave differently in fabric st ages.

7.4.2 The Principle of Non-conventional Spun Yarn / 新型纺纱原理

The structure of yarns from new spinning systems differ from that of ring spun yarns. Although detailed discussions are provided in the following lectures, the basic structural features of the yarns from major new spinning technologies are provided.

7.4.2.1 Rotor Spinning / 转杯纺

In rotor spinning, the fibers are added to the yarn tail continuously almost one at a time, with the result that the fibers exhibit individual helix structure.

The yarn structure will have two distinct regions, namely the core characterized by helical twisting of fibers and, the sheath constituted by individual or a thin ribbon of wrapper fibers, which form belts on the yarn surface. The belts may be wrapped loosely or tightly with varying sense of twist.

The rotor spun yarn, therefore, has 'Bipartite Structure', which exhibit differential twist.

As the rotor spun yarn has bipartite structure the core exhibits twist structure more or less similar to that in ring spun yarns and the sheath is characterized by belts having varying intensity and direction of wrapping.

The fiber in the core are twisted helically with the fibers near the yarn axis showing low helix angle while those near the surface have greater helix angles. Further since the fibers are attached to the yarn tails almost one at a time, the fibers exhibits individual position with a wide range of helix angles. The mean helix is angling around 35 degree. The wrapper fibers also show wide range of variation in respect of tightness and direction of wrapping over the yarn length. Due to this reasons it is evident that the rotor spun yarns exhibits differential twist structure (Fig. 7-9).

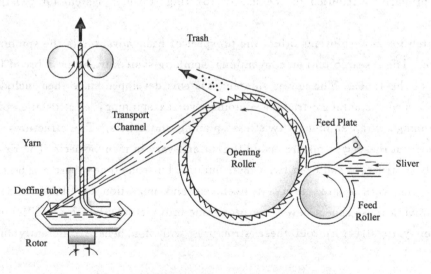

Fig. 7-9　Main features of rotor spinning system

7.4.2.2　Air-jet Spinning / 喷气纺

Yarn manufacture using the air jet primarily produces fascinated yarns using the false twist principle. Hence, we discuss about the principle of false twisting before going into actual air jet spinning.

The air-jet spinning system with distinct way of yarn formation results in the production of unique structure.

The air-jet-spun yarn is fascinated yarn consisting of a core of parallel fibers held together by wrapper fibers.

The structure of air-jet-spun yarn is essentially that of comparatively straight central core of fibers held together by taut surface fibers wound onto the central core helically. The straight fibers termed as "core fibers" while the taut, helically fibers called as "wrapper fibers" (Fig. 7-10).

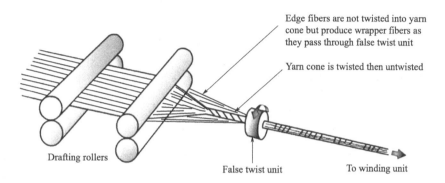

Fig. 7-10　Dupont system of air-jet spinning

7.4.2.3　Friction Spinning / 摩擦纺

A friction spun yarn appears like a ring spun yarn visually, but its internal structure differs from that of ring spun yarn or rotor spun yarn.

The yarn is characterized with inferior fiber orientation and loose packing of fiber in the cross section.

The structure of friction spun yarn varies depending upon mode of yarn formation like DREF 2 and DREF 3.

The internal structure of open-end friction spun yarn is characterized by inferior fiber orientation, buckled and folded fiber configurations and loose packing of the fibers associated with low tension during yarn formation (Fig. 7-11).

The degree of fiber orientation and extension is so low that the fibers of 40 mm length can be found in 10 mm long section in case of DREF 2 and in DREF 3. The fiber extent of sheath of yarn is 19 mm which corresponds to 50% fiber length utilization of fiber of 38 mm and for core structure the fiber extent is 32 mm for 38 mm fiber length which gives spinning coefficient of 0.85. DREF 3 yarn has good fiber extent as compared to DREF 2 yarn.

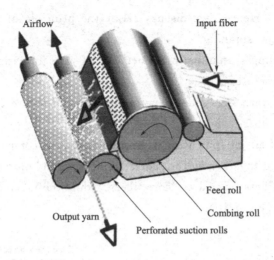

Fig. 7-11　Priciple of friction spinning

7.4.2.4　Vortex spinning / 涡流纺

Vortex spinning technology was introduced by Murata Machinery Ltd. Japan in 1997. This technology is best explained as a development of air-jet spinning, making use of air jets for yarn twisting.

The basic principle of operation is shown in Fig. 7-12. The sliver is fed to 4-over-4 (or a four-pair) drafting unit. As the fibers come out of the front rollers, they are sucked into the spiral-shaped opening of the air jet nozzle. The nozzle provides a swirling air current which twists the fibers. A guide needle within the nozzle controls the

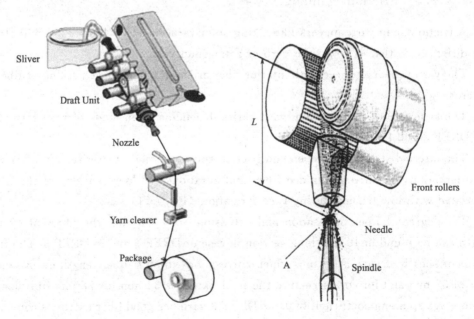

Fig. 7-12　Principle of Vortex spinning

movement of the fibers towards a hollow spindle. After the fibers have passed through the nozzle, they twine over the hollow spindle. The leading ends of the fiber bundle are drawn into the hollow spindle by the fibers of the preceding portion of the fiber bundle being twisted into a spun yarn. The finished yarn is then wound onto a package.

7.4.2.5 Air-Vortex Spinning / 气流涡流纺

In this spinning method (Fig. 7-13), yarn is formed by an air vortex in a tube ①. For this purpose, air is sucked by a vacuum source ⑥ into the tube through tangential slots ②. This incoming air moves upward along the tube wall in a spiral and finally arrives at the upper tube seal ③. Since the top of the tube is closed by the seal ③, the air then flows to the center of the tube and moves down again to the vacuum source. Thus an air vortex ⑤, rotating continuously in the same direction, is generated at the seal ③.

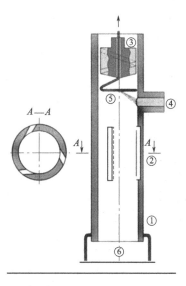

Fig. 7-13 The principle of Air-Votex spinning

Opened fiber material is allowed to enter the system through a tangential opening ④. The rising air stream grasps this material and transports it upward into the vortex ⑤. To form a yarn, an open yarn end is passed into the tube through a passage in the upper seal ③. The vortex grasps this yarn end and whirls it around in circles in the same way as the fibers. Since the upper yarn length is held by the withdrawal rollers and the lower end is rotating, each revolution of the yarn end in the vortex inserts a turn of twist into the yarn.

7.4.2.6 Electrostatic Spinning / 静电纺

The principle of electrostatic spinning is shown in Fig. 7-14. In this process, a roving ② taken from the roving frame ① is passed to a conventional double-apron drafting arrangement ③ and is subjected to a draft of up to 80-fold. The fibers exit freely from the front cylinder. They must then be collected to form a fiber strand and twisted to form a yarn. The first of these operations is performed by the electrostatic field, and twisting is carried out in a twist-imparting unit ⑥. Twisting presents no problems. The complexity of this method lies wholly in the electrostatic field generated between the front roller and the twist element ⑥ by earthing the front roller and applying a high voltage (about 30 000~35 000V) to the twist element. This field has to accelerate the fibers ④ and guide them toward yarn end ⑤ while maintaining the elongated configuration of the fibers. When the fibers enter this field, they take up charge and form dipoles, i. e.: one end becomes positively charged and the other negatively charged. An open yarn end ⑤ projects from the twist element into the field. This yarn is negatively charged and is therefore always attracted to the front roller. Due to the dipole pattern, there is thus a relatively high degree of fiber straightening between the front roller and the twist element. Fibers leaving the roller are accelerated and attracted to the yarn as a result of the charges carried by the two parts. They join continuously to the yarn. Since the yarn rotates, the fibers are bound in. A yarn is formed continuously and is withdrawn by withdrawal rollers ⑦, to be passed to a take-up device ⑧ for winding onto a cross-wound package.

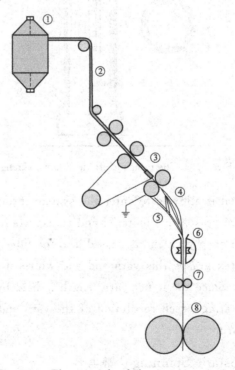

Fig. 7-14　The principle of electrostatic spinning

7.4.3 The Pros and Cons of New System Yarn / 新型纺纱的特点

(1) Main problems

① Yarn character differing from that of ring-spun yarn, which still represents the basic standard for comparison.

② Characteristics occasionally bordering on the unusable.

③ Difficulties in maintaining consistently uniform yarn characteristics.

④ Greater demands on the raw material.

⑤ Market segments limited to: a narrow count range, specific raw material types, specific end products.

⑥ A high level of process know-how, and expenditure on repair and maintenance.

(2) Advantages

① High production rates.

② Elimination of processing stages.

③ A considerable reduction in: personnel and space.

④ Relative ease of automation.

Glossary of Technical Terms / 专业词汇:

picking	清棉，摘棉
scutching	清棉
trash	杂质
picker	清棉机，摘棉机
card sliver	生条，粗梳条子
first drawframe	头道并条机
taker-in	(梳棉机) 刺辊
cylinder	锡林，滚筒
fillet	针布，弹性针布
mote knife	除尘刀
undercasing	漏底
strip	剥取
staple	U形钉
flat	盖板
doffer	道夫
condensing trumpet	凝聚喇叭口
coiler	圈条器
can	条筒
combing	精梳 (工艺)
detaching roller	分离罗拉

noil	精梳落棉（毛）
doubling	并合
ring	钢领
ring frame	环锭细纱机
slubbing frame	头道粗纱机
sliver can	条筒
roving	粗纱
roving frame/flyer frame	粗纱机
flyer	锭翼
finisher drawing	末道并条
bobbin	筒管
open-end spinning	自由端纺纱
rotor spinning	气流纺纱，转杯纺纱
vortex spinning/air vortex spinning	涡流纺纱
air-jet spinning	喷气纺纱
friction spinning	摩擦纺纱
self-twist spinning	自捻纺纱
rotor	纺纱杯，纺杯，转杯
pill	起球
oxford	牛津布
DREF spinning	德雷夫纺纱法，尘笼纺纱法

Questions / 思考题：

1. Why is cotton blended with polyester for dress making material?
2. What is the importance of twist for a yarn?
3. How many types of yarn twist are you aware of?
4. What is the measure of yarn twist?
5. How does twist affect the fabric properties?
6. Explain the process of drawing.
7. At which stage of yarn manufacture is twist introduced in cotton?
8. Describe the principle of non-conventional spun system.

Activities / 实践作业：

Describe in detail the process of conversion of cotton fiber to yarn in your study group and introduce the corresponding frames in our training workshop.

Chapter Eight
Weaving and Woven Fabrics / 机织与机织物

Objectives / 学习目标：

1. Define the terms: woven fabric, warp yarn, weft yarn.
2. Describe the main characteristics of the three basic weaves.
3. State the purpose of weaving preparation.
4. Describe the operation of a loom.
5. State the development of the shuttleless looms.

8.1 Introduction to Fabrics / 织物概述

Some years ago the terms cloth and fabric were interchangeable. They were usually defined as materials made by weaving, knitting, or felting fibers. Today this definition is no longer satisfactory. Fabrics can be made without the use of fibers, as in vinyl upholstery; or they can be made by other processes, as in nonwoven disposable or liners.

Now we define a fabric as any thin, flexible material prepared from cloth, polymeric film, foam, directly from fibers, or any combination of these methods. A cloth is any thin, flexible material prepared from yarns. By these definitions, such materials as wallpaper, plastic upholstery products, carpets, and nonwoven materials are fabrics; woven, knit, tufted, or knotted materials made from yarns are cloth. Note that cloth is a fabric, but all fabrics need not be cloth.

8.2 Construction of Woven Fabrics / 机织物结构

Weaving is the oldest method of producing cloth. Although the machinery for weaving cloth has changed over the millennia, the basic operation has remained the same. Weaving, which is the interlacing of two or more sets of yarns (usually at right angles to each other), requires holding one set of yarns in parallel rows and passing another set over and under the first set. The set of lengthwise yarns is called the warp, and the individual warp yarns are known as ends. The set of crosswise yarns is the fill or filling. The individual fill yarns are called picks. (Other names for the filling are weft). To keep the cloth from unraveling, a narrow width at each edge is closely woven. This strip is called the selvage. The closeness of the weave is determined by the yarn count (also called the thread count), which is defined as the number of ends and the number of picks per square inch of cloth (Fig. 8-1). Yarn count may be given as the sum of the warp and fill yarns, or as the number of warp yarns by the number of fill yarns. For example, a sheeting material may be described as 140 count, or as 77×63 muslin. The higher the yarns count, the closer the cloth construction.

Woven structures may be conveniently divided into two principle categories, as follows:

(1) Simple structures

In which the ends and the picks intersect one another at right angles and in the cloth are respectively parallel with each other. In these constructions there is only one series of ends and one series of picks and all the constituent threads are equally responsible for

Chapter Eight Weaving and Woven Fabrics / 机织与机织物

(a) Light fabrics

(b) Middle thick fabrics

(c) Heavy fabrics

Fig. 8-1 Woven fabrics

both the aspect of utility or performance and aesthetic appeal in a fabric.

(2) Compound structures

In which there may be more than one series of ends or picks some of which may be responsible for the "body" of the fabric, such as ground yarns, whilst some may be employed entirely for ornamental purposes such as "figuring", or "face" yarns. In these cloths some threads may be found not to be in parallel formation one to another. There are many pile surface constructions in which some threads may project out at right angles to the general plane of the fabric.

Until the early nineteenth century, weaving was a hand craft. In the late 1700s and early 1800s, inventors and engineers such as Joseph Marie Jacquard and Edmund Cartwright developed looms that were partially machine powered. Gradually, power looms replaced hand looms for commercial manufacturing, although hand looms conti nue to be manufactured for hand weaves.

8.3 The Three Basic Weaves / 三原组织

The three basic weaves (plain, twill, and satin) can be made on the simple loom without the use of any attachment.

8.3.1 Plain Weave / 平纹组织

Plain weave is the simplest of the three basic weaves that can be made on a simple loom (Fig. 8-2). It is formed by yarns at right angles passing alternately over and under each other. Each warp yarn interlaces with each filling yarn to form the maximum number of interlacing. Plain weave requires only a two-harness loom and is the least expensive weave to produce. It is described as a 1/1 weave: one harness up and one harness down when the weaving shed is formed. Plain weave fabrics have no right or wrong side unless they are printed or given surface finish. Their plain, uninteresting surface serves as a good background for printed designs, for embossing, and for pucke red and glazed finishes. Because there are many interlacings per square inch, plain weave fabrics tend to wrinkle more, ravel less, and be less absorbent than other weave. Interesting effects can be achieved by the use of different fiber contents, novelty or textured yarns, yarns of different sizes, high or low twist yarns, filament or staple yarns, and different finishes.

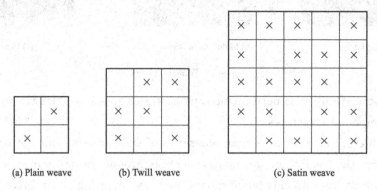

(a) Plain weave　　　(b) Twill weave　　　(c) Satin weave

Fig. 8-2　Basic weaves

The simplest form of plain weave is one in which warp and filling yarns are the same size and the same distance apart so they show equally on the surface balanced plain weave. Other forms have warp yarns so numerous as to cover the filling that are obvious only in the form of ridges called ribs—unbalanced plain weave, and variations that have two or more yarns interlaced as one—basket weave.

8.3.2　Twill Weave / 斜纹组织

Twill weave is one in which each warp or filling yarn floats two or more filling yarns with a progression of interlacings by one to the right or the left to form a distinct diagonal line or wale (Fig. 8-2). A float is that portion of a yarn that crosses over two or more yarns from the opposite direction. Twill weaves vary in the number of harnesses. The more complex twills may have as many as 18 picks inserted before repeating and are woven on a loom with a dobby attachment. Twill weave is the second basic weave that can be made on the simple loom.

Twill weave is often designated by a fraction (for example 2/1) in which the numerator indicates the number of harnesses that are raised and the denominator indicates the number of harnesses that are lowered when a filling yarn is inserted. The fraction 2/1 would be read as "two up, one down". The floats on the surface are warp yarns making it warp surface, so called warp-faced twill.

(1) Even-sided twills

Even-sided twills have the same amount of warp and filling yarn exposed on both sides of the fabric. They are sometimes called reversible twills because they look alike on both sides although the direction of the twill line differs. Better quality filling yarns must be used in these fabrics than in the warp-faced twills since both sets of yarn are exposed to wear. They are 2/2 twills and have the best balance of all the twill weaves.

(2) Warp-faced twills

Warp-faced twills have a predominance of warp yarns on the right side of the cloth. Since warp yarns are made with higher twist, they are stronger and more resistant to abrasion.

The major advantages of a twill fabric are that it is durable and wears well, resists soiling, and has good resistance to wrinkling. Its disadvantages are that, once soiled, it is more difficult to clean than plain-weave fabrics, and it usually has a right and wrong side, which may make garment design difficult. Unless given special treatments, some uneven twill fabrics produce garments that are prone to twisting or skewing on the body after laundering.

8.3.3 Satin Weave / 缎纹组织

Satin weave (Fig. 8-2) is one in which each warp yarn floats over four filling yarns (4/1) and interlaces with the fifth filling yarn, with a progression of interlacings by two to the right or left. (or each filling yarn floats over four warps and interlaces with the fifth warp (1/4) with a progression of interlacings by two to the right or left). In certain fabrics, such as double damask and slipper satin, each yarn floats across seven yarns and interlaces with the eighth yarn. Satin weave is the third basic weave that can be made on the simple loom, and the basic fabrics made with this weave are satin and sateen.

Satin-weave fabrics are characterized by luster because of the long floats that cover the surface.

When warp yarns cover the surface, the fabric is a warp-faced fabric satin and the warp count is high. When filling floats cover the surface, the fabric is a filling-faced.

All these fabrics have a right and wrong side. A high yarn count gives them strength, durability, body, firmness, and wind repellency. Fewer interlacings give pliability and resistance to wrinkling but may permit yarn slippage and raveling.

8.4 Weaving Process / 机织过程

Weaving process can be divided into two parts: preparation for weaving and weaving on the loom.

8.4.1 Preparation for Weaving / 织造准备

Although the mechanisms of forming woven and knitted fabrics are very different, nevertheless, they both have one common factor, yarn. Both systems manipulate yarns to produce a fabric.

Yarns as manufactured and packaged are not in the optimum condition to be used to form fabrics. After yarn formation, both spun and continuous filament yarns are not immediately usable in fabric forming systems. Package size, build and other factors make it necessary for the yarn to be further processed to prepare it to be handled efficiently during the fabric formation.

For weaving and warp knitting, many yarns are presented simultaneously in the form of a warp sheet. These yarns are taken from packages called beams. Shuttle looms need a special filling yarn package, or quill, which fits in the shuttle; while shuttleless looms and weft knitting machines use yarn from large packages called cheeses or cones.

From the above it can be seen that the yarn, packaged as it comes from spinning, is virtually useless. It must be repackaged to meet the particular needs and demands for the fabric forming system in which it is to be used. This, in fact, is one of the functions of yarn preparation, to put the yarn on a suitable package for a particular fabric forming system.

(1) Winding

The first step in yarn preparation is winding. The reasons for winding yarns are: ① to produce a package which is suitable for further processing, and ② to inspect and clear the yarn (remove thick and thin spots). To perform the above tasks a winder is divided into three principle zones: the unwinding zone, the tension and clearing zone, and the winding zone. After winding, warp yarns are wound on cones for warper creels and weft yarns are wound on pirns which fit into shuttles.

(2) Warping

This is the process by which a fixed number of cones of yarns in a warper creel are wound on to a beam. If the fabric forming system is weaving or warp knitting, some or all of the yarns forming the fabric are presented in sheet form. It is necessary therefore to remove the yarns from the winding package and arrange the desired number on a package called a beam. The yarns must be parallel and under uniform tension. This, then, is the purpose of warping.

(3) Slashing

This is to strengthen the warp yarns by coating them with size, so that they may not break during weaving. In the weaving process, the warp yarns are subjected to rubbing and chafing against metal by being threaded through drop wires, heddles and reed; they are constantly being rubbed together during shedding; they are subjected to tension both constant, by the let-off and take-up, and intermittent, by the shedding and beat-up. All of these lead to conditions which are favorable to end breakage, an occurrence which should be minimized. Thus, it is desirable to produce as high a quality warp as possible, one which will withstand the rigors of weaving. This is the purpose of slashing or warp sizing.

(4) Drawing-in

This is to draw-in the warp ends after slashing through the reed splits. Whether the weave from design paper will be produced in the woven fabric depends upon this process.

8.4.2 Weaving on the Loom / 织造

8.4.2.1 Traditional Loom / 传统织机

Weaving is done on a machine called a loom. All the fabrics that are known today have been made by the primitive weaver. The loom has changed in many ways, but the basic principles and operations remain the same.

The Industrial Revolution and mass production cause changes in looms, all of which were aimed at achieving high speed production. The basic modern loom consists of two beams, a weaver's beam and a cloth beam, holding the warp yarns between them. As can be seen in the two-harness loom as one harness is raised, the yarns form a shed through which the weft yarn can be inserted (Fig. 8-3).

Fig. 8-3 Shuttle loom

Previous to weaving, the warp threads must be placed side by side just as they will be in the fabric and wound on to a beam. The length of these threads must, of course, be approximately that of the fabric to be woven. Also the weft thread will be wound on small cops. Since the weft thread has to be moved between the warp threads in weaving, it is not possible to make these cops large, so a large number of these have to be used one after the other in making a long length of fabric.

The warp beam (or weaver's beam), which holds the lengthwise yarns, is located at the back of the machine and is controlled so that it releases yarn to the weaving area of the loom as needed. This function is the let-off motion, the first of four primary loom motions. The heddles are wire or metal strips that allow control of the individual ends; an end is pulled through the eye located in the center of each heddle. The individual heddles are mounted in a harness that allows the warp yarns to be controlled in groups. A loom has at least two harnesses, and most have more. The number of harnesses on a loom helps determine the complexity of the fabric design that can be produced.

In a two-harness loom, every other warp yarn across the width of the fabric is in one harness. When that harness is raised, half of the warp yarns rise to produce an opening between the two sheets of warp yarns. This opening known as the shed produces a path through which the filling is inserted. The loom motion is called shedding and the order in which harnesses are raised and lowered produces a pattern in the fabric. In looms containing more than two harnesses, the sequence for drawing ends through heddles and mounting heddles in harnesses becomes more intricate. In many cases, groups of harnesses are raised and lowered together. A very good fabric designer is needed to plan the drawing-in of a warp and the sequencing of harness movements in a 32-harness loom.

The third basic loom motion is picking or filling insertion. For many years, filling yarns was laid across the shed with a shuttle. In today's weaving machines, another devices such as a jet of air or water, a rapier, or a small projectile, is used to place the pick. Then each filling yarn must be packed against the previously placed pick. This is accomplished by using a reed, which is parallel to the harness, to press the pick into position. This is the beat-up motion, the fourth loom motion.

The cloth beam, or cloth roll located at the front of the loom, holds the completed fabric; as each pick is beaten into position, the fabric just produced is rolled onto the take-up beam. This take-up motion is the final loom motion, because let-off and take-up occur simultaneously, the loom motion is usually referred to as "let-off and take-up".

Most fabrics are produced on weaving machines with eight or fewer harnesses; elaborate fabrics, however, require many harnesses and the special attachments required to control groups of harness, or they have mechanisms similar to computer controls that move each individual warp yarn to produce complex patterns.

8.4.2.2 Shuttleless Loom / 无梭织机

For centuries, the basic loom operated with a shuttle to lay the filling, or picks. The speed with which the shuttle is sent back and forth is limited by the mass of shuttle—usually about 200 picks per minute. Manufactures have long sought a way to replace the shuttle and increase the speed of weaving.

Shuttleless looms were developed as a way without the shuttle. Because they both increased productivity and lowered noise levels, they were widely adopted. Shuttleless weaving machines wove 17 percent more fabric in 1987 than they did in 1982, and Textile World predicts that shuttle loom will be outnumbered by shuttleless weaving machines in the early 1990s. The major types of shuttleless looms are water jet, air jet, rapier and projectile loom. In all four types of looms the filling yarns are measured and cut, thus leaving a fringe along the side. This fringe may be fused to make a selvage, if the yarns are thermoplastic, or the ends may be turned back into the cloth. These selvages are not always as usable as conventional selvages because of a tendency toward puckering that requires slitting.

(1) Water-Jet Loom

The water-jet loom uses a high pressure jet of water to carry the filling yarn across the warp (Fig. 8-4). It works on the principle of continuous feed and minimum tension of the filling yarns, so it can weave fabrics without barre or streaks. The filling yarn comes from a stationary package at the side of the loom, goes to a measuring drum that controls the length of each filling, and continuous by going through a guide to the water nozzle, where a jet of water carries it across through the warp shed. After the filling is carried back, it is cut off. If the fibers are thermoplastic, a hot wire is used to cut the yarn, fusing the ends so they serve as a selvage.

The water is removed from the loom by a suction device. Water from the jet will dissolve regular warp sizing so one of the problems has been that of developing water-resistant sizing that can be removed easily in cloth finishing processes. The fabric is wet when it comes from the loom and must be dried (an added expense).

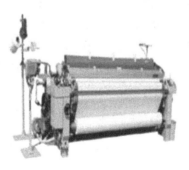

Fig. 8-4 Water-jet loom

The loom is more compact, less noisy, and takes up less floor space than the conventional loom. It can operate at 400 to 600 picks per minute—two or three times faster than the conventional loom. Maintenance is relatively easy.

(2) Air-Jet Loom

Air-jet weaving (Fig. 8-5) is more popular because the machines cost less to purchase, install, operate, and maintain than rapier or projectile weaving machines, and the air jet can be used on a broader variety of yarns than a water jet.

Fig. 8-5 Air-jet loom

The yarn is pulled from the supply package at a constant speed, which is regulated by the rollers, located with the measuring disk just in front of the yarn package. The measuring disk removes a length of yarn appropriate to the width of the fabric being woven. A clamp holds the yarn in an insertion storage area, where an auxiliary air nozzle forms it into the shape of a hairpin.

The main nozzle begins blowing air so that the yarn is set in motion as soon as the clamp opens. The hairpin shape is stretched out as the yarn is blown into the guiding channel of the reed with the shed open. The yarn is carried through the shed by the air currents emitted by the relay nozzles along the channel. The maximum effective width for air-jet weaving machines is about 355cm. At the end of each insertion cycle the clamp closes, the yarn is beaten in, then cut, after the shed is closed. Again, some selvage-forming device is required to provide stability to the edge of the fabric.

The loom can operate at 320 picks per minute and is suitable for spun yarns. There are limitations in fabric width because of diminution of the jet of air as it passes across the loom.

(3) Rapier Loom

The rapier system (Fig. 8-6) operates with either flexible or rigid metal arms, or rapiers, attached at both sides of the weaving area. One arm carries a pick to the center of the weaving area; the arm extending from the other side grasps the pick and carries it across the remaining fabric width. Newer rapier machines are built with two distinct weaving areas for two separate fabrics. On such machines, one rapier picks up the yarn from the center, between the two fabrics, and carries it across one weaving area; as it finishes laying that pick, the opposite end of the rapier picks up another yarn from the center, and the rapier moves in the other direction to lay a pick for the second weaving area, on the other half of the machine.

Fig. 8-6　CL736 Rapier Loom

Rapier looms weave more rapidly than most shuttle looms but more slowly than most projectile machines. The rapier-type loom weaves (primarily) spun yarns at 300 picks per minute. An important advantage of rapier looms is their flexibility, which permits the laying of picks of different colors. They also weave yarns of any types of fiber and can weave fabrics up to 110 inches in width without modification. This loom has found wide-acceptance for use with basic cotton and wool worsted fabrics.

(4) Projectile Loom

The projectile loom (Fig. 8-7) uses a small bullet-shaped projectile with a gripper that pulls the yarn off the supply package at the side of the weaving areas and carries it across the shed. Only enough yarn for one pass across the width of the fabric is carried across. Projectile looms with one or more projectiles are available; the multiple-projectile type is more common. The single-projectile system picks up yarn on the supply side and carries it the entire width of the shed. After beat-up has occurred, the projectile picks up yarn from a second supply source on the other side and returns across the shed to place the next pick.

Multiple-projectile systems can be used in machine with a wide weaving bed so the projectile grippers can transfer the pick across the fabric in a relay fashion. In other multiple-projectile systems, the gripper from the first projectile picks up yarn from the supply source and moves across the shed to lay that length of yarn; then, as beat-up occurs, the projectile drops into a conveyor system that returns it to the supply side to pick up new yarn in the meantime, the second gripper has pulled a pick to repeat the process.

Each pick is individually cut, so there is not a continuously woven selvage like that

Fig. 8-7　P7300 Projectile Loom

produced by a shuttle machine. Instead, the edges are fringed. To finish them, a tucking device is used on both sides to interlace the fringe with the last few warp yarns along each edge.

8.5　Technical Parameters of Woven fabrics / 机织物结构参数

8.5.1　Piece-Length / 匹长

Fabric piece-length is determined by fabric applications, weight, thickness, packing capacity and so on. Generally, fabric piece-length is between 27m and 40m. United pieces are 2-3, 3-4 and 4-6, in heavy fabrics, middle thick fabrics and light fabrics, respectively.

8.5.2　Fabric Width / 幅宽

Fabric width is determined by the required fabric, such as patterns repeat, weave repeat, color arrangement, etc..

8.5.3　Fabric Density / 织物体积密度

Fabric density is important in fabric comfort. It may be expressed in the following formula:

$$\text{Density}(g/cm) = \text{fabric weight}(g/m^2 \text{ or } g/cm^2) \times \text{thickness}(cm)$$

8.5.4　Fabric Count / 织物经纬密度

In a piece of woven fabric, usually there are more warp yarns than filling yarns. The closeness or looseness of the weave is measured by the count of the cloth, which is determined by the number of picks or ends the square inch. For example, if the count

Chapter Eight   Weaving and Woven Fabrics / 机织与机织物

of the cloth is 276×254, which can be also expressed as 276 warp yarns and 254 filling yarns per 10cm.

8.5.5　Fabric Weight / 单位面积质量

In general, woven fabric weight is the combined weight of the warp and the filling yarns. It determines to a great extent the weight of the end-use product. Woven fabric can be sorted into light fabric, heavy fabric and middle thick fabric. Fabric weight is commonly calculated in g/m^2 or oz/yd^2.

Glossary of Technical Terms / 专业词汇：

disposables	用可弃；用可弃产品
vinyl	乙烯基
upholstery	室内装潢，室内装饰
liner	衬垫；衬里
woven fabric	机织物
knitted fabric	针织物
tufted fabric	簇绒织物
knotted fabric	网罗织物
warp/ends	经向，经纱
filling/weft/picks	纬纱，纬向
unraveling	脱散，散边
selvage	布边
yarn count	纱线支数；织物密度
thread count	织物经纬密度
muslin	平纹细布，薄纱织物
body	身骨
ornamental	装饰的
ground yarn	地纱，底纱
face yarn	面纱，正面纱线
pile	绒头，绒毛；毛圈
loom	织机
plain	平纹，平纹组织
twill	斜纹，斜纹组织
satin	缎纹，缎纹组织
attachment	附件，配件
harness	综，综丝
weaving shed	织造梭口，梭道
right side	织物正面

wrong side	织物反面
print	印花，印刷
surface finish	表面整理
embossing	凹凸轧花，浮雕印花，压花，拷花
puckered finish	起皱整理
glazed finish	高光泽（轧光或摩擦轧光）整理
wrinkle	起皱，皱纹
ravelless	不易散开
absorbent	吸水剂
novelty yarn	花式纱线
rib	棱纹，凸条
basket weave	方平组织
float	浮线
progression	连续浮起
wale	凸条纹，纹路清晰的斜纹
dobby	多臂
warp-faced twill	经面斜纹
even-sided twill	双面斜纹
reversible twill	双面可用斜纹
wear	穿，使用，磨损
double damask	双锦缎
slipper satin	鞋面花缎
sateen	棉缎
preparation	准备
heddle eye	综眼
interlace	交织
harness	综丝
harness frames	综框
reed-split	筘隙
shuttle	梭子
design paper	意匠图
braid	编带，辫子
draw-in	穿经纱
size	浆料，上浆
drawing-in	穿筘
firmness	坚固，牢固性
creel	筒子架
shuttleless loom	无梭织机

pirn	纡子，纡管，纬纱管
let-off	送经运动
beam	经轴，织轴
take-up	卷取运动
slashing	浆纱（工序）
beat-up	打纬运动
cone	锥形筒子
shedding	梭口，开口
warper	整经机
weaver	织布工
breast beam	胸梁
cop	纡子，纬管
back rest	后梁
cloth roller	卷布辊
warp beam	经轴，织轴
weaver's beam	经轴，织轴
heddles	综丝
opening	开口
shed	梭口
rapier	剑杆
projectile	片梭
reed	筘，钢筘
picker stick	投梭棒
water-jet loom	喷水织机
air-jet loom	喷气织机
rapier loom	剑杆织机
projectile	片梭
fringe	毛边
selvage	布边
puckering	绉纹
slitting	切口，切割
barre	纬向条花
streak	条痕，织物
nozzle	喷嘴
sizing	上浆
water-resistant	抗水的
suction device	吸水装置
gripper	夹子，片梭；夹纱器

Questions / 思考题：

1. What are woven fabrics?
2. What is the thread count of a woven fabric?
3. Compare the main characteristics of the three basic weaves.
4. Give examples of the uses of the three basic weave.
5. Why the yarn preparation is necessary?
6. Why the shuttle looms will be replaced by the shuttleless looms?
7. What are the five main motions in a weaving machine?

Activities / 实践作业：

1. Visit your local department stores and apparel shops. Make an inventory of the plain, rib, basket, twill, and satin weave constructions in the following end uses:

    a. Junior sportswear   b. Men's suits   c. Women's daytime wear

Can you account for the preponderance of one construction over the others in each of the categories? Explain.

2. Visit your local department stores and apparel shops. Make an inventory of fabric constructions and fiber types used in men's and women's wear. Does one constructions or fibers dominate?

Chapter Nine
Knitting and Knit Fabrics /
针织与针织物

Objectives / 学习目标：

1. Define the terms: count, course, wale, gauge, stitch.
2. Distinguish the difference between warp-knit fabrics and weft-knit fabrics.
3. State the three basic weft-knit constructions.
4. State the main characteristics of the major weft-knit structures.

Knitting is defined to be the formation of fabric by the intermeshing of loops of yarn. In machine knitting, loops of yarn are formed with the aid of needles or shafts. As new loops are formed, they are drawn through previously formed loops. This continuous formation of new loops and interloping produces a knit fabric.

9.1 Terms of Knitting and Knit Fabric / 针织和针织物的基本术语

Several terms are specific to knitting and knit fabrics. The following definitions refer to the technical face of the fabric.

① Count the total number of wales and courses in a square inch of knitted fabric.

② Course a horizontal row of successive loops, comparable to the filling yarns of woven fabric.

③ Gauge the fineness or coarseness of the fabric, determined by the number of needles (or stitches) per unit width on the machine. It is usually expressed as eedles per inch or needles per centimeter. On single jersey machine, cut is often used to express needles per inch. The higher the cut, the more stitches per inch.

④ Stitch the loop formed at each needle; the basic unit of knit fabric structure.

⑤ Wale a vertical row (or column) of loops produced by an individual needle. Wale run parallel to the longer dimension of a knit fabric and indicate the machine direction of the fabric; they are comparable to the warp yarns of woven fabrics.

⑥ Warp knit a knitted fabric in which the yarn producing the loops in the fabric is carried the length of the fabric, that is, in the lengthwise or warp-direction.

⑦ Weft knit a knitted fabric in which the yarn producing the loops in the fabric is carried across the width of the fabric, that is, in the crosswise, or weft direction.

9.2 Weft Knitting / 纬编

In weft knitting, the loops of yarn are formed by a single weft thread. The loops are formed, more or less, across the width of the fabric usually with horizontal rows of loops, or courses, being built one loop at a time. Each yarn is fed at more or less a right angle to the direction in which the fabric is built. The term weft is taken from weaving terminology. In weaving the term is used synonymously with filling or pick to refer to the crosswise yarns that are laid during the weaving operation.

Weft knit fabrics can be made by machines, weft knitting is also the technique usually used in hand-knitting. A considerable amount of filling knit fabric is made on a circular knitting machine, in which a series of needles is arranged around the circumference of a circle. Fabric may be made in the shape of a tube. If a flat fabric is desired, the tube can be cut open. Many fabrics, in fact, are made with a specific location for

Chapter Nine Knitting and Knit Fabrics / 针织与针织物

slitting the fabric open. Such knits could not be used in tube form. Other circular knits are designed so that they may be used in the cylinder or tube form in which they are made, adjustments are made for shaping to a figure or form for end use.

Knitting machines used for weft knitting may also be of the flat bed type. In these the needles are arranged parallel to each other in a flat plane. Flat bed machines that are used to make ribbed knit fabrics having two sets of needles arranged to form a V shape with the open end of the V parallel to the base of the machine.

The major characteristics of weft knits are:
① they can be either fully fashioned or cut, to shape and sewn;
② they form a run in the length-wise, or wale, direction if a loop or yarn breaks;
③ they have good stretch, especially in the course direction;
④ they do not ravel;
⑤ they are available in a wide variety of constructions and patterns;
⑥ they do not wrinkle easily and have good recovery from wrinkling and folding.

The three basic weft-knit constructions are: jersey, rib, and purl.

The simplest of the knit cloths is the jersey or plain knit. In this pattern all the stitches are brought toward the face of the fabric. The jersey is the basic pattern for knit goods. The reasons for this are:
① the cloth has relatively good stretch in both lengthwise and widthwise directions;
② the cloth recovers most of the stretch so that it is not easily pulled out of shape;
③ the cloth can be sewn without great difficulty. In addition, it is easy to make on relatively in expensive machinery.

The disadvantages of jersey include a tendency to unravel when snagged or pulled, little run resistance when the yarns are torn or cut, a propensity to shrink when laundered, and a tendency to curl when patterns are cut out.

Jersey knits are used for sweaters, underwear, hosiery, dresses, and sport shirts.

Purl-knit cloth, which has a rather nondescript appearance, is made by alternating course of knit and purl stitches. Purl knits provide fabrics of the same bulk as jersey of the same weight. Furthermore, this cloth provides fair stretch recovery in the wale-wise direction, but can be stretched out of shape in the course-wise direction. This makes it best suited to stoles, scarves, quilts, and other items that are not subject to crosswise stretching; its utility for garments is limited because of its poor shape retention.

Rib knits are made by alternating wales of knit and purl stitch. The rib stitch appears as a series of hills and valleys running lengthwise across the surface of the cloth. In the simplest construction the wales alternate as knit purl. However, more complex combinations may be formed, as in a 2/1 or a 2/3 rib. Rib knits with an even repeat such as 1/1 or 2/2, are reversible.

Rib-knit cloth provides greater bulk than jersey of the same weight. It also provides excellent elasticity in the coursewise direction. For this reason, the rib is used for cuffs and collars to provide a body-fitting closure for neatness and protection against the wind. Rib knits do not curl as jersey knits do, so cutting and sewing is not as difficult. However, because of the ease with which the cloth stretches, care must be taken in construction. Since one of the desirable properties of rib-knit garments is the close fit they provide, some shrinkage is tolerable. Because of this, such garments may be laundered. This easy-care feature has helped enhance the popularity of rib-knit fabrics.

9.3 Warp Knitting / 经编

The term warp knitting is also adapted from weaving technology. Machines used for warp knitting tend to look somewhat like weaving machines. All of the yarns are placed on the beams and are located behind and above the actual knitting area. All yarns feed into the knitting area at the same time. Each yarn is manipulated by one specific needle as the interloping proceeds; however, guide bars control the placement of the yarn, and the particular needle forming the loop may vary from one interlooping action to the next. Jacquard attachments can be used to provide for special needle controls and the making of highly patterned warp knits.

Warp-knit fabrics are tighter, have less stretch, and are not as bulky as weft knits. Furthermore, warp-knit fabrics have better dimensional stability, greater resistance to snagging, raveling, running, and abrasion, as well as higher strength than weft knits. Warp knits are also prized for their soft hand, smoothness, sheerness, and good draping qualities. The warp-knit cloths of major importance are tricot and raschel.

Tricot fabrics are characterized by lengthwise wales on the face and diagonal cross yarns on the back. The major types of tricot fabrics are plain tricot (or tricot jersey), satin tricot, brushed or napped tricot. Plain tricot fabric, produced primarily from filament yarns on machines equipped with two guide bars, is the simplest formation and the most widely used. Satin tricot is a tricot variation characterized by a smooth, satiny finish on the effect (face) side of the fabric, which is really the technical back. Brushed tricot is produced with a brushing operation to create a napped surface on one side of the fabric.

In both warp and weft knitting, the principal mechanical elements used to form loops are needles. The most common type of needles, used in both warp and weft knit-

Chapter Nine Knitting and Knit Fabrics / 针织与针织物

ting, is the latch needle. The latch needle, developed in the mid 1800s, is so named because it can be closed using a latch which is activated without any special assistance during the knitting process.

Glossary of Technical Terms / 专业词汇：

intermesh	线圈相互穿套
loop	线圈
course	线圈横列
wale	线圈纵列，凸条纹
gauge	隔距，织针号，针号
stitch	组织，线圈，针迹
jersey knits	平针织物
purl knits	双反面针织物
shape retention	保形性
rib knits	罗纹针织物
stole	女式披肩
tricot	经编织物，经平组织
run resistance	防脱散性
resistance to snagging	防勾丝性
raschel	拉舍尔针织物
plain tricot	经平组织
satin tricot	经缎组织
brushed tricot	经绒组织
sheerness	透明度，细薄度
latch needle	舌针
needle hook	针钩
knockover	脱圈
held loop	握持线圈
sinker	沉降片
weft knitting	纬编针织物
warp knitting	经编针织物
circular knitting	针织圆机
flat bed knitting	横机
needle bar	针床，针座
guide bar	导纱梳栉，（经编机）梳栉

Questions / 思考题：

1. What are the difference between weaving and knitting?

2. What are the characteristics of weft knits?
3. What are the characteristics of warp-knit fabrics?
4. Why the jersey knits is most widely used?

Activities / 实践作业：

Visit your local department stores and apparel shops. Make a inventory of the knitted fabrics as they are used for apparel and home furnishings. Where and how are they used? What advantages do they offer?

Chapter Ten
Nonwoven Fabric / 非织造布

Objectives / 学习目标：

1. Define the term nonwoven fabric.
2. State the development of the nonwoven fabrics.
3. State the basic sequence of steps in manufacturing nonwoven fabrics.
4. State the main methods of web formation.

Nonwovens are sheet or web structures made by bonding fibers, yarns, or filaments by mechanical, thermal and solvent means. Bonding fabrics are one category of nonwoven fabrics as currently defined. This group includes fabrics formed from a web of fibers held or bonded together by an applied adhesive, the use of a solvent to soften or dissolve a component of the web, or softening of fibers by heat.

Contemporary nonwoven fabric dates back to the early 1930s. At that time, a few textile companies began experimenting with bonded materials as a way of utilizing cotton waste. The first commercial production of the products now called nonwovens began in 1942 in the United States in an effort to produce fabric directly from fiber. The market for nonwoven products has experience tremendous growth and has potential for more.

Nonwovens may be classified as either disposable or durable goods. Disposable, or nondurable, nonwovens include such one-time-use products as diapers, medical dressings, household wipes, and disposable protective clothing. Durable goods are used for apparel interfacings, automobile headliners, road underlayments, and carpets.

The basic sequence of steps in manufacturing nonwoven fabrics is as follows:
① preparation of the fiber;
② web formation;
③ web bonding;
④ drying and curing.

Most bonded fiber fabrics are sold in an unfinished state. If dyeing and finishing are involved, they become the fifth step.

Modern bonded fiber fabrics are no longer produced from waste fibers only. Although a small percentage of waste is still used, manufacturers have turned increasingly to good-quality fibers. Furthermore, while early bonded products were made of cotton, today's bonded fabrics utilize almost any type of fibers or combination of fibers. The length of fibers varies from 1/2 inch to 2 inches, and some structures are actually fused filament fibers. Since there is no yarn spinning involved, fibers of different lengths and different chemical compositions can be successfully combined in a desired cost and performance of the end product. Fiber webs can be formed by either dry-lay or wet-lay procedures.

10.1 Dry-lay Webs / 干法成网

In dry-lay, there are three processes; these techniques of web formation involve oriented, cross-lay, and random fiber arrangements. Oriented webs are those in which the fibers are parallel to the longitudinal axis. They can be formed on cotton or wool cards. Cotton cards result in uniform webs and fabrics with a texture similar to that of woven cloth. However, the production rate is low. Wool cards and garnetts produce webs at a rapid speed, but the web is less uniform. All webs of the oriented group are comparatively weak in the direction perpendicular to the lay of the fibers.

Cross-lay webs are made by combining two layers of fibers at right angles to each other. They are expensive to produce and no more satisfactory than random webs. Consequently, this technique is seldom used.

Random web formation is steadily gaining popularity with manufacturers largely because special machines have been developed. The introduction of such unit as the Random-Webber accelerated production of random-web nonwovens. The machine employs an air-doffer principle. It is described as air-lay systems.

The air-doffer principle involves the spreading and laying of fibers by controlled air currents. Air suction pulls the fibers from the supply or feeder rolls or belts and deposits them in a random arrangement on a condenser roll. The fiber mat is then fed into a compressor, which forms the fabric. Advantages of this method include uniformity in thick-ness, equal strength in all directions, and reasonable cost of manufacture.

After the web is formed, bonds between the fibers must be strengthened and stabilized.

Bonding techniques employed in bonding fiber webs formed by the dry-lay process include belows.

① An adhesive or bonding agent, either a dry powder or a liquid, is applied directly to the web in a separate step. The power is usually a thermoplastic substance that is fused into the web by the application of dry heat. If a wet solution used, it is spread uniformly over the web and then set by chemical action or heat.

② Thermoplastic fibers are uniformly blended in the fiber mix and are evenly distributed within the web. Heat is applied, and the thermoplastic fibers soften and fuse over and around the other fibers. As the web cools, the fibers are all held firmly toge ther.

The adhesive technique is most commonly used. These methods behave differently on different fibers or fiber blends, so the manufacturer must have considerable technical knowledge to make the right choice of bonding agent for the specific end-used of each fabric type.

10.2 Wet-lay Webs / 湿法成网

Bonded fiber fabrics may be formed as fibers are deposited from a suspension in water. This is the technique used in making paper; it has been adopted by some manufacturers to form fabrics. The main difference is in the length of fiber used; paper uses very short fibers, whereas these fabrics are made from fibers between 1/4 and 1/2 inch in length.

One important reason for the use of wet-lay system is economy. Fabrics can be formed more rapidly and, hence, more economically than by other techniques. The general procedural steps are belows.

① Web formation. Fibers are suspended in water, then deposited from the suspension onto a special type of support, where the water is removed.

② Bonding. The bonding agent may be incorporated into the suspension in the form of either adhesive or binder fibers. The adhesives seal the fibers together as they dry; the binder fibers have special properties that cause them to react and seal or bind other fibers into a cohesive fabric. Fibers used for this include special-formula polyvinyl alcohol fibers and special viscose fibers. Wet-lay webs of fibers may be bonded by applying an adhesive to the newly formed web and drying and curing.

Bonded fiber fabrics appear in a number of products. They are found in diapers, handkerchiefs, skirts, dresses, apparel interfacings, bandage, and shrouds. Other typical products include curtains, decontamination clothing, garment bags, industrial apparel, lampshades, map backing, napkins, place mats, ribbon, upholstery backing, window shades, carpeting, and blankets.

A major defect of bonded fiber fabrics for apparel is their lack of good draping qualities. The fabrics tend to be firm and somewhat stiff. A further problem is their lower strength as compared with woven or knitted fabrics of comparable weight. However, continued growth in bonded fiber fabric production and application is a certainty because of economy in production.

Glossary of Technical Terms / 专业词汇:

dry-lay web	干法成网
cross-lay	交叉铺放
random fiber arrangement	无定向纤维排列，无定向铺放
garnett	锯齿开松机，弹毛机
Random-Webber	兰多制网机
air-doffer	气流成网
fiber mat	纤维网
suspension	悬浮液
binder fiber	黏结用纤维，纤维状黏合剂
cohesive fabric	黏合织物
polyvinyl alcohol	聚乙烯醇
apparel interfacing	衣服衬头
decontamination cloth	防污染服装

| place mat | 餐具垫子 |
| carpeting | 地毯料 |

Questions / 思考题：

1. What are the basic steps in making the bonded fiber nonwovens?

2. Compare the three methods of dry laid web formations.

3. What are the main characteristics of the wet process?

4. What limitations do nonwoven fabrics have? Take examples of the end uses of nonwoven fabrics.

Activities / 实践作业：

Collect examples of nonwoven fabrics, conclusion the end uses of nonwoven fabrics.

Chapter Eleven
Care Labels and Textile Standards / 洗涤标签与纺织标准

Objectives / 学习目标：

1. State the history of care label.
2. Describe the two key goals of care labels.
3. Understand the requirements of care label in China.
4. What are textile standards?
5. What are the Chinese mandatory national (GB) standards?
6. Which standard do textile and apparel products put up for sale in China must comply with?

11.1　Care Labels / 洗涤标签

11.1.1　A Brief History of Care Labels / 洗涤标签的发展史

Long before polyester, acrylic and automatic washing machines came along, consumers could easily identify a wool or cotton garment and successfully clean it without a care label.

But those days are long gone. New fibers and new technology have created a vast array of apparel and textiles—each designed to look beautiful and to stand up to the test of time. Unfortunately, consumers had no way of knowing just how to properly clean these items, often damaging both the apparel's beauty and long-lived nature.

So in 1972, the Federal Trade Commission introduced the Care Labeling Rule which, for the first time, required manufacturers to label their clothing with instructions for at least one safe cleaning method for the garment. From this time on, it would be considered unfair and deceptive for manufacturers or importers to sell items without care labels.

11.1.2　Two Key Goals of Care Labels / 洗涤标签的关键作用

Requiring care labels actually accomplished two very important goals. First, it helped consumers make buying decisions based upon the care method required. Some people prefer the convenience of dry cleaning, others the economy of machine washing. At the same time, care labels assured that consumers knew how to safely clean their clothes so that they retained their appearance and performance over time. Something which the entire apparel industry was all for as well.

11.1.3　The Requirements of Care Label in China / 中国洗涤标签的要求

The labels on textile products should be in the Chinese characters and include the following mandatory data:

① name and address of the manufacturer;
② name of the product (in accordance with Chinese standard);
③ size (in accordance with standard GB 1335);
④ product composition: name and composition of the various raw materials used;
⑤ cleaning instructions (compulsory use of symbols defined by GB/T 8685—2008—SGS information sheets are available in English and in Chinese);
⑥ storage conditions and other recommendations: compulsory for delicate pro ducts;

⑦ 'best before' date (only for products that are perishable);

⑧ N°of standard;

⑨ quality classification (if required by Chinese standard).

The labels also have to respect the following presentation, according to the product:

① printing or direct weaving in the fabric;

② label sewn, or affixed or hanged to the product;

③ printing or pasted to the packaging;

④ in the documents accompanying the product.

Information including the model, type, and specifications of the product, product composition and cleaning instructions must be affixed in a permanent label. For fabrics, the label can be either hanged, printed, or woven.

11.1.4 The FTC Rule / FTC 规则

(1) The Trade Regulation Rule

It is an unfair method of competition and an unfair or deceptive act or practice to sell, in commerce, any textile product in the form of a finished article of wearing apparel, or piece goods made for the purpose of immediate conversion by the ultimate consumer into a finished article of wearing apparel, which is not accompanied by a label or tag which clearly discloses instructions for the care and maintenance of such products.

Both manufacturers in the United States and importers are covered by the regulation.

Several exemptions are defined in the published rule.

① Totally reversible wearing apparel without pockets.

② Products where appearance or usefulness would be harmed if the label were attached, and the manufacturer of the product specifically request an exemption for that product.

③ For items exempt under "a" and "b", the consumer must be provided with a conspicuous hang tag or package labeling which can be seen before buying the product.

④ When items may be cleaned safely under the harshest procedures and there is reliable proof that all of the following washing and dry-cleaning procedures may be used on the product.

machine washing in hot water;

machine drying at a high setting;

ironing at a hot setting;

bleaching with all commercially available bleaches;

dry cleaning with all commercially available solvents.

⑤ Products sold to institutional buyers for commercial use.

The manufacturer or importer must establish a reasonable basis for care information. They must have reliable evidence that the procedures recommended on the label will not harm the item. That evidence may consist of current technical literature, past experience, a record that a fair sample of the product was tested, or other reliable information.

For the purpose of this rule, a **care label** is defined as "a permanent label or tag, containing regular care information and instructions, that is attached or affixed in such a manner that it will not become separated from the product and will remain legible during the useful life of the product."

Certain piece goods means "textile products sold by the piece from bolts or rolls for the purpose of making home sewn textile wearing apparel." This includes remnants, the fiber content of which is known, that are cut by or for a retailer but does not include manufacturers' remnants, up to 10 yards long, that are clearly and conspicuously marked pound 'goods' or 'fabrics of undetermined origin' and trim, up to 5 inches wide.

Textile wearing apparel means "any finished garment or article of clothing made from a textile product that is customarily used to cover or protect any part of the body, including hosiery, excluding footwear, gloves, hats or other articles used exclusively to cover or protect the head or hands."

In general, labels for textile wearing apparel must have either a washing or a dry-cleaning instruction. If a product may be either washed or dry-cleaned, the label has to have *only one* of the instructions. If the product cannot be cleaned by any available cleaning method without being harmed, the label must give that information.

Washing instructions include descriptions of washing, drying, ironing, and bleaching. If any part of the washing procedure that the consumer can be reasonably expected to use would harm the product or any other items being washed with it, the label must contain a warning to this effect. Clear warning words are "Do not," "no," and "only." Warnings are not necessary for any procedure that is an alternative to the one described on the label. For example, if a label says "Dry, flat," it is not necessary to give the warning "Do not tumble dry."

The terms used in washing instructions must adhere to specific guidelines outlined in the regulations. The label must state whether the product should be washed by hand or machine and give the water temperature that may be used. If the regular use of hot water (up to 150°F) will not harm the product, the label need not mention any water temperature. The term "machine wash" means a process by which soil is removed from products in a specially designed machine using water, detergent or soap, and agitation.

Drying instructions must indicate whether the product should be dried by machine or some other method. If machine drying is called for, the label must state a drying temperature that may be used unless the use of a high temperature will not harm the product. Ironing must be mentioned on a label only if it will be needed on a regular basis to preserve the appearance of a product. If a product will be harmed by ironing, the label should state "Do not iron." If ironing is mentioned and no temperature is given, it is assumed that the regular use of a hot iron will not harm the product.

If all commercially available bleaches may be used, the label need not mention bleaching. If commercially available bleaches would harm the product, the label must say "No bleach" or "Do not bleach." If the use of chlorine bleach would harm the product, but a nonchlorine bleach would not, the label must say "only nonchlorine bleach when needed."

Dry cleaning means "a commercial process by which soil is removed from products or specimens in a machine which uses common organic solvent (e. g., petroleum, perchlorethylene, fluorocarbon). The process may include adding moisture to the solvent, up to 75 percent relative humidity, hot tumble drying up to 160°F and restoration by steam press or steam-air finishing."

If a dry-cleaning instruction is given, the label must state at least one type of solvent that may be used unless all commercially available solvents may be used, in which case the label need not mention a type. The terms "dry-cleanable" and "commercially dry-clean" may not be used in an instruction. The term "professionally dry-clean" may be used to ensure optimum results either by a dry-cleaning attendant or through the use of a dry-cleaning machine that permits solvent modifications, or both.

A warning must be given against using any part of the dry-cleaning procedure (that consumers or dry cleaners could reasonably be expected to use) that would harm the product or others being cleaned with it. For example, if a product can be dry-cleaned in any solvent but steam should not be used, the label should state "Professionally dry-clean. No steam."

(2) Synopsis

It is important to remember, when reading an FTC-required care label, that

① Only the washing or dry-cleaning process specified in the instruction has been checked for safe use.

② If no temperature is mentioned, it is safe to use any temperature or setting.

③ If no ironing instruction is given, it should not be necessary to iron the product.

④ If bleach is not mentioned, any type of bleach may be used.

⑤ If no warnings are given, there is no need to make adjustments to the care process given on the label.

A common complaint from consumers regards the ongoing use of what is termed "low-level labeling." Garments continue to be labeled "Dry-clean" when a washing procedure would not adversely affect them; or "Hand wash, warm" is used when the garment could be machine washed safely. The manufacturer is required to attach a label for a "safe" care instruction, and many of them prefer to provide a label that gives the procedure least likely to produce damage.

11.1.5 International Care Symbols / 国际标准洗涤标志

The International Standards Organization (ISO) has recommended the international adoption of a system of care symbols to replace written instructions. Where apparel is manufactured in a country, speaking one language and sold in countries speaking other languages, such a system of symbols is helpful. Bilingual countries and regions find symbols easier to deal with than instructions written in two languages. Currently the Federal Trade Commission does not recognize the use of care symbols as an appropriate method of care labeling in the United States.

The symbols that have been adopted for use in other countries are shown in Fig. 11-1. Many residents of the United States purchase clothes made abroad that contain these labels. It is difficult to understand the symbols because they are seldom explained in consumer publications in the United States. In areas where the symbols are used routinely, however, laundry product containers and washing machines include explanations of the symbols.

The code basically consists of the following symbols, each of which is variable.

The washing Process   A number and a temperature in the wash tub symbol indicates that the article can be washed safely either by machine or hand. The figure which appears above the waterline in the tub represents the full washing process and the figure below the waterline represents the water temperature. The symbol may be accompanied by a box containing a written description of the process. There are nine numbered processes in the international code but only seven are likely — to be used in the UK. These can be seen in detail on most washing product packets.

A hand in the wash tub indicates that the articles must not be washed by machine. The appropriate hand wash instructions may be added in a box alongside the symbol.

The wash tub crossed out indicates that the article must not be washed.

Only the letters A, P and F are recognized. In some circumstances the circle containing P or F may be underlined. This indicates that special procedures are required as these goods are sensitive to dry cleaning.

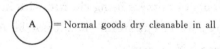 = Normal goods dry cleanable in all solvents. cleaning.

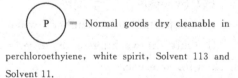 = Normal goods dry cleanable in perchloroethyiene, white spirit, Solvent 113 and Solvent 11.

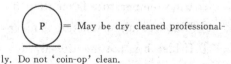 = May be dry cleaned professionally. Do not 'coin-op' clean.

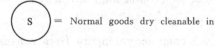 = Normal goods dry cleanable in white spirit or Solvent 113.

Chapter Eleven   Care Labels and Textile Standards / 洗涤标签与纺织标准

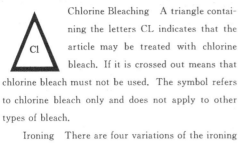

Chlorine Bleaching   A triangle containing the letters CL indicates that the article may be treated with chlorine bleach. If it is crossed out means that chlorine bleach must not be used. The symbol refers to chlorine bleach only and does not apply to other types of bleach.

Ironing   There are four variations of the ironing symbol. The temperatures shown in brackets are the maximum sole plate temperature indicated by the dots in the symbol.

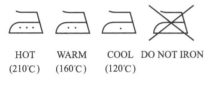

HOT (210℃)   WARM (160℃)   COOL (120℃)   DO NOT IRON

Drying   The vast majority of textile articles can safely be tumble dried. Care labels may be used to indicate either that tumble drying is the optimum drying method for a particular article, or that tumble drying should not be used if the article is likely to be harmed by this treatment.

In cases where the tumble drying prohibition symbol is used, any special positive instructions, such as "dry flat" for heavier weight knitwear, should be given in words.

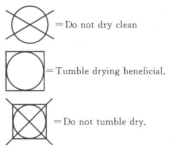

= Do not dry clean

= Tumble drying beneficial.

= Do not tumble dry.

Fig. 11-1   Suggested international Sure-Care symbols

11.2   Textile Standards / 纺织标准

11.2.1   Introduction of Textile Standards / 纺织标准简介

Textile standards provide the specifications and test methods for the physical, mechanical, and chemical properties of textiles, fabrics, and cloths, as well as the natural and artificial fibers that constitute them. The textiles covered by these standards are commonly formed by weaving, knitting, or spinning together fibers such as glass fiber strands, wool and other animal fibers, cotton and other plant-derived fibers, yarn, sewing threads, and mohair, to name a few. These textile standards help fabric and cloth designers and manufacturers in testing textiles to ensure acceptable characteristics towards proper end-use.

11.2.2   Textile Standards of China / 中国纺织标准

Textile and apparel products put up for sale in China are subject to certain quality and safety requirements, identified as mandatory national (GB) standards, as well as various and professional standards.

Professional standards (also called industry standards) apply when no national GB standard exists. Professional standards are sector-specific technical or quality requirements. The code "FZ" is used for textile sector standards and the code "QB" for light industry, which includes leather, fur and feather products. Voluntary standards are indicated with "/T" added after the codes.

In addition to national standards and professional standards there also may be local standards (often referred to as "provincial standards"), and/or enterprise standards.

Textile and apparel products put up for sale in China must comply with GB 18401—2010 "National General Safety Technical Code for Textile Products". GB 18401 contains the principal requirements, test methods, and test rules for textile products in China's market. Also, Textile and apparel products put up for sale in China must be labeled, as required by GB 5296.4 "Instruction for Use of Products of Consumer Interest—Instructions for Use of Textiles and Apparel".

Glossary of Technical Terms / 专业词汇：

dry clean	干洗
do not dry clean	不可干洗
compatible with any dry-cleaning methods	可用各种干洗剂干洗
iron	熨烫
iron on low heat	低温熨烫
iron on medium heat	中温熨烫
iron on high heat	高温熨烫
do not iron	不可熨烫
bleach	可漂白
do not bleach	不可漂白
dry	干衣
tumble dry with no heat	无温转笼干燥
tumble dry with low heat	低温转笼干燥
tumble dry with medium heat	中温转笼干燥
tumble dry with high heat	高温转笼干燥
do not tumble dry	不可转笼干燥
dry	悬挂晾干
hang dry	随洗随干
dry flat	平放晾干
line dry	洗涤
wash with cold water	冷水机洗
wash with warm water	温水机洗
wash with hot water	热水机洗
handwash only	只能手洗
do not wash	不可洗涤

Chapter Eleven Care Labels and Textile Standards / 洗涤标签与纺织标准

mandatory national (GB) standards	国家标准
professional standards/industry standards	行业标准
voluntary standards	推荐性标准
local standards/provincial standards	地方标准
enterprise standards	企业标准

Questions / 思考题:

1. What is dry cleaning? What advantages does dry cleaning over home laundering? Survey what articles should be so cleaned.

2. List some testing subjects for textiles.

Activities / 实践作业:

1. Search textile standards via internet

You may search for various national GB standards on China's Standardization Administration (SAC) website. Search by entering the product standard number or title. Or, try entering a general product name (e. g., raw silk) for the title to get a list of relevant standards. Compulsory GB standards are provided for free by the SAC in Chinese.

Standards are also available at the American National Standards Institute (ANSI) eStandards Store, which allows users to browse and purchase Chinese National GB Standards or American standards.

2. Collect some labels of your clothes, compare the including with each other.

Reading Material 1
Textured Yarns / 变形纱

The production of man-made fibers results in filament yarns that are very smooth and strong. However, these yarns have a limited amount of stretch, very low bulk, and practically no hairiness; all these factors are important in defining the comfort of garments. For these reasons, manufacturers developed techniques for improving the comfort potential of their yarns.

Texturing increase the potential elongation of yarns by converting the straight filaments into various crimped or curled configurations. Thus, cloth made from these yarns stretches more and allows greater freedom of motion to the wearer. Texturing also increases the bulkiness of yarns; the bulkier yarns yield of fabrics that have an improved ability to trap air, so cloth made from these yarns is warmer.

The air and moisture permeability of the cloth is increased. In the absence of wind, air is trapped within the yarns and provides warmth. However, because the filaments of the yarns are separated by the texturing process, a breeze can penetrate the cloth. The overall effect of texturing is to make the cloth feel warmer in winter and cooler in summer.

By crimping or curling the filaments, texturing allows the filament yarns to feel more like spun yarns. The hairiness of the spun yarn is approximated by the projections of the loops and the curves of the crimps. The cloth does not lie flat against the skin, but is supported by these projections. The garment provide a more pleasant tactile sensation to the wearer.

In addition to its effect on comfort, texturing also provides subjective improvement to the finished cloth. The bulkier yarns give the cloth a firmer body. Thus, garment do not hang limply, but fall in pleasing folds. The hand is improved. Consumers report a more pleasant, warmer, less synthetic feel to cloth after the yarns have been textured. The appearance of the goods is improved. Light reflection is more diffuse, giving the cloth a muted luster and a more attractive appearance.

Ease of maintenance is affected in two ways. The textured yarns, being more elastic than the untreated filament yarns, proved improved wrinkle resistance. However, since the filaments are generally produced from wrinkle-resistant fibers, this effect is small. Of greater importance is the tendency of textured yarns to soil more readily because they are more open and provide a coarser surface than untextured yarns.

The abrasion resistance of textured yarns is slightly decreased, because the filaments are separated from each other. The individual filaments cannot aid each other as readily in resisting abrasive forces, so individual fibers are more easily broken.

In sum, textured yarns improve the comfort and appearance of cloth prepared from them. This improvement is, however, purchased at the cost of decreased resistance to soiling. Durability of the fabric is hardly affected by the texturing process.

Reading Material 2
New Types of Loom / 新型织机

CL736 Rapier Loom

CL736 Rapier Loom is mainly used for light and heavy fabrics produced with cotton, wool and mixed yarns. It can accommodate 16~20 heddles.

The crank shaft is driven by the pulley that is driven by motor via motor pulley and three triangle belts.

The picking system is a 6-lever weft leading mechanism. The rotation of the big eccentric wheel is driven by the crank shaft. The wheel swings up and down over picking system, and forces triangle pendular arm to move up and down. Because the fulcrum of the triangle pendular arm is fixed on the wall plate, the front fulcrum is initiated vertical motion, making the lower pulling fulcrum to swing back and forth around the rocker shaft. Hence, the sector gear plate drives the gear on the rapier transfer box to push the weft through the formed shed. Since the 6-lever weft picking stroke is short, the rapier stroke outside the selvage is also short. And the time of the left and the right rapiers coming out of the selvages can be adjusted.

The beating-up system is 4-lever short pulling form. In the operation, the crank shaft is linked with the sley bracket installed on the rocking shaft. When the crankshaft rotates, the crank arm and pulling out unit drive the sley bracket to swing forth and back, and the reed installed on the sley bracket finishes beating-up motion.

The machine can meet with the process requirement of various fabrics with different width. And various twill, Khaki drill and figured cloth can be weaved on the machine.

P7300 Projectile Loom

In the projectile loom, grippers grip the end of the filling yarn to finish the filling yarn insertion. Projectile looms made in Sulzer textile machinery from Swiss are widely used in China.

The crank shaft is driven by V-shape belt pulley which is linked with the motor installed the left wall. The crank shaft crosses over the beating-up boxes, each box having a couple of conjugate cams, which are driven by the loom to finish the beating-up motion. The driving equipment of the projectile loom consists of belt pulley, clutch mechanism, switching mechanism and anti-reverse-rotation device.

P7300 projectile loom may be at most equipped with ten or fourteen pieces of conjugate cams. Torsion bar is turned to make elastic energy stored and the connecting-bar is in dead point. And the place of the dead point of picking cam is destroyed to release the elastic energy. So, the energy pushes the gripper through the shed. Beating-up motion is carried out by the reed connected with conjugate cams. The function of the reed is to provide the gripper fly to the shed. Electronic letting-off and taking-up devices are developed into functional integration.

Narrow-width and broad-width fabrics, light, heavy and middle thick fabrics, pure color and multicolor fabrics, and plain or complex patterns fabrics can be produced on P7300 projectile loom.

Fluid Jet Loom

Fluid Jet Loom mainly includes air jet loom and water jet loom. Both them use a highly pressure jet of air or water to carry the filling yarns across the shed. The drawback of the former is that the air diffuses quite rapidly so that the width of the woven fabric is limited. However, in water jet loom, water diffuses much more slower than air. So, if wider fabrics need to be produced, auxiliary nozzles and other guides should be used to ensure the filling yarns carried through the shed. It is noted that the yarns made from chemical fibers are appropriated in water jet loom because hydrophilic sizes used to the warp yarns during slashing can be dissolved by water.

Reading Material 3
Mechanical Bonding / 机械固结

Mechanical bonding is the oldest method of producing nonwovens; it entangles fibers to impart strength to dry-laid webs. The most common mechanical methods are needle punching and spunlacing, also called hydroentangling.

(1) Needle Punching

In needle punching, barbed needles are punched vertically through the web to hook and entangle tufts of fibers. Needle-punched nonwoven resemble felt in appearance, but they are made primarily from fibers other than wool. Characterized by high density combined with some bulk, they are available in weights from 50 to 285 grams and in thickness from 15 to 160 mils.

Two basic steps are involved in the construction of needle-punching nonwovens:

① The fiber web, or batt, prepared by either carding, garneting, or air-laying techniques, is fed into a machine with specially designed needles.

② The batt moves on a substrate between a metal bed plate and a stripper plate; the needles punch through the plates and the fiber web, reorienting the fibers so that mechanical interlocking or bonding occurs among the individual fibers.

The substrate may be filaments, a scrim, or some other form. Placement of the substrate in the middle of the fiber web improves the strength and structural integrity of the finished needle-punched fabric.

The strength of needle-punched fabrics also depends on the fiber arrangement within the webs. If fibers are placed parallel to each other, the finished fabric will have good strength in that direction but will tend to be weak in the opposite direction. If the fibers are in a random arrangement, strength is equal in all directions. A two-step process first tacks the web with 30 to 60 punches per square inch and then punches with 800 to more than 2500 penetrations per square inch. The higher number of punches is used for fabrics such as blankets, which are expected to be subjected to considerable handling during use and care.

The properties of needle-punched fabrics depend on the length and characteristics of the fiber or fibers, the physical properties of the web, and the techniques used to produce the web. Most needled fabrics lack any structural pattern because the needles punch and intermingle the fibers in such a random way that the fabric surface appears uniform. Needle-punched fabrics produced with a modified needle bed and needles that penetrate beyond the surface to form loops on the back can be made to resemble loop pile, velour, or velveteen. The loops either are left uncut or are cut and brushed to give the surface appearance of the pile-woven fabric.

Needle-punched fabrics frequently are found in carpeting and other floor coverings, wall coverings, blankets, padding material, insulation materials, industrial fabrics, and fabrics for vehicles.

(2) Hydroentangling

In hydroentangling or spun lacing the fibrous web is subjected to high-velocity water jets to entangle the fibers, causing them to curl and knot around each other. These materials are produced without a binder, resulting in lightweight, soft, and drapable spun-lace fabrics. The Nexusi fabrics by Burlington, available in several patterns that can be dyed or printed, best typify this group. Some of these fabrics are washable, others are dry-cleanable. Fabrics range in weight from 0.7 to 2.2 ounces per square yard and in thickness from 3.5 to 25 mils. Typical end uses include quilt-backing fabrics, mattress pad ticking, substrates for coated fabrics of various types, interlinings, curtains, table coverings, and selected items of apparel. Although most of the spun-laced fabrics on the market are made of polyester, it is possible, to use other fibers.

Reference / 参考文献

[1] Marjory L. Joseph. Introductory to Textile Science [M]. 15th ed. Holt, Rinehart and Winston: The Dryden Press, 1986.
[2] Corbman, Bernard P. Textiles: Fiber to Fabric [M]. 6th ed. New York: McGraw-Hill, Inc., 1983.
[3] Joseph J. Pizzuto. Fabric Science. 5th. New York: Fairchild Publications.
[4] Lawrance CA. Fundamentals of Spun Yarn Technology [M]. London: CRC Press, 2003.
[5] Mary Humphries. Fabric Reference [M]. 3rd ed. New Jersey: Person Education, Inc., 2004.
[6] 上海纺织工业局《英汉纺织工业词汇》编写组. 英汉纺织工业词汇 [M]. 北京: 中国纺织出版社, 1992.
[7] 李建萍. 纺织专业英语 [M]. 成都: 四川大学出版社, 2005.
[8] 托托拉, 默克尔. 仙童英汉双解纺织词典 [M]. 第7版. 黄故等译. 北京: 中国纺织出版社, 2004.